Alan Robson – the highest-paid radio presenter outside London – has determinedly stayed in the North despite offers to join Radio 1. He is the front man for Metro FM, and broadcasts six days a week on the 'Night Owls' phone-in programme. He also has a page in the *Sunday Sun*, the North's bestselling Sunday paper.

SIMPLY THE BEST
Geordie Jokes and Stories

Also by Alan Robson

Grisly Trails and Ghostly Tales

Simply the Best

ALAN ROBSON

Virgin

First published in Great Britain in 1992 by
Virgin Books
an imprint of Virgin Publishing Ltd
338 Ladbroke Grove
London W10 5AH

The moral right of the author has been asserted

A catalogue record for this title is available from the
British Library

ISBN 0 86369 673 2

Phototypeset by Intype, London
Printed and bound in Great Britain by
Cox & Wyman Ltd, Reading, Berks

This book is dedicated to all my friends who were kind enough to offer their support.

Special thanks to Barry Hunter and Rob Shreeve for their invaluable support, and to all at Virgin Publishing.

CONTENTS

FOREWORD

Northern humour is famous all over the world, yet no one has ever really put down on paper the real jokes, stories and anecdotes from the people of the North East. As a comedian in my early days, through to my years on radio and television, I have gathered together hordes of material, some of which is collected in this book.

Although it covers stories about the entire North, my beloved patch – from the Scottish Borders to the North Riding of Yorkshire, Cumbria to the North East coast – it is called *Simply the Best Geordie Jokes and Stories*.

If you describe a bloke from Sunderland a Geordie he'll redesign your face; call a Yorkshireman a Geordie and you'll be enjoying hospital food – so strong are the identities of each of the areas concerned. Yet to those north of the Scottish border, those south of Yorkshire, and certainly those in foreign parts, anyone in our patch is a Geordie. This is the Northerners' joke book, put together by a Northerner for the North.

The boring old stereotype of a Northerner is someone who can drink seventy bottles of Newcastle Brown Ale every week, plants leeks, races

1

whippets, digs coal and can build a ship. The truth is that the North is now a buzzing modern region, with new industries (hopefully) growing, the biggest and most innovative shopping centre in Europe, the most castles, finest beaches and best scenery in all of Britain. The North Yorkshire Moors, the Lake District, Northumberland, Durham City, York – the list is endless.

Northern actor Brendan Healey said it all on *Robson's People* on Tyne Tees Television: 'When I'm in London I rip down all of the posters advertising the Northern tourist boards. We don't want people to find out how really great it is up here. We don't want them spoiling it for the rest of us!'

So let's put a grin across your chops with a tonic for you, wherever you come from.

THE NORTHERNER –
BORN TO BE ROMANTIC

To many Northerners foreplay means shouting, 'Brace yourself, Hinny!', but here is a selection of romantic interludes that sum up the invention that comes after following the stirrings buried deep inside the underpants.

The pub called the Three Mile Inn is on the edge of Gosforth, one of the trendier and rather more money-soaked suburbs of Newcastle, and one day a poser called Peter popped in for a white wine. Whilst he stood at the bar he saw a young lass sitting all on her own in the corner. He flashed her a smile, and she sent it right back at him. He motioned to her that he'd like to buy her a drink and she shook her head, saying, 'No, I don't drink. My Mam told me that it damages your health and stops you from thinking straight.'

He was impressed with her high standards, bought some 'fizzy watter' (Perrier) and sat down beside her. He offered her a cigarette and once again she refused, saying, 'Oh no, tobacco is bad for you. Nicotine is addictive, and passive smoking

3

is harmful too so I must insist you don't smoke either!' He was really pleased to find a genuine and caring lady with a solid moral stand.

Around 9.30 p.m. he was beginning to feel peckish, so he asked if she would care for a bar meal. She politely refused, saying, 'I am three pounds over my recommended weight so I must refuse, but don't let me stop you!' Over his steak sandwich he mused at how fortunate he was to find someone so considerate who also wanted to look after her tremendous figure.

So at closing time he offered to drive her home and as he stood outside her house he hinted that he'd like to be asked in.

'Yes, you can come in,' she replied. 'Just remember I do not believe in pre-marital sex, so I am merely inviting you in for a coffee, to say thank you for such a wonderful and stimulating evening.'

Peter was thrilled. Surely this was the girl of his dreams – she was beautiful, intelligent, caring, she didn't smoke, she didn't drink, she didn't overindulge and she was still a virgin.

Then she opened the door and there in the passage was a dead horse. Peter's mouth just fell open, and she added, 'I never said I was tidy, did I?'

*

One day Albert from the local video shop suspected that his wife was having an affair, so he decided not to go to work and instead hid down the street and watched the house. Almost an hour later an XR3 pulled up, and out hopped this man in jeans and a polo shirt and in he went.

Albert waited ten minutes, then burst into the house. He looked in the living room but there's no

4

sign of them, so he bounded up the stairs like a man possessed and kicked open the bedroom door.

'Where is he?' he yelled.

His beautiful blonde wife, lying naked in the bed, asked, 'Where's who?'

But Albert knew he was there, so he proceeded to search the house. Finally on opening the wardrobe, there was the man, stark naked except for his socks.

'So what are you doing in *my* wardrobe?' barked Albert.

Thinking quickly, the man says, 'Oh, I am the moth inspector. I heard you had trouble with moths, so I came to check it out.'

Albert added, 'So what are you doing with no clothes on then?'

The man looked down at himself and said, 'The little buggers!'

*

Northern women are rampant! One day a salesman arrived in Blyth and found himself a small bed-and-breakfast place. It was the middle of winter, so the only people there were the owners and their beautiful daughter Karen. As the night progressed the parents went to bed, leaving the salesman in the TV lounge with their daughter. As salesmen tend to be perpetually randy, he reached over and tried to hold her hand. 'Stop,' she yelled, 'or I'll tell my dad on you!'

A little while later he leaned over and attempted to kiss her ear. 'Stop,' she yelled, 'or I'll tell my dad on you!'

On his third attempt she melted into his arms, and they rolled about the sofa making mad

5

passionate love. After a wonderful time she snuggled up to the salesman and said, 'Shall we try that again?' He duly obliged.

They snoozed awhile, then she gently shook him saying, 'Shall we go for a hat trick?' So the salesman rallied to the cause and they made love again.

About twenty minutes later she shook him, saying she wanted more. 'Stop,' cried the salesman, 'or I'll tell your dad on you!'

*

Money has been tight in the North for years, particularly for old-age pensioners, yet a wonderful thing happened in 1983. A member of Monaco's millionaire fraternity was passing through the West End of Newcastle when he realised that he had to buy some stamps, so he parked his limousine in Clara Street, and walked round to the Post Office. The place was packed with old folk queueing for their pensions, and the millionaire felt really sorry for the old man and woman in front of him. Both of their pensions couldn't have added up to £70. A tank of petrol for his limo cost more than that, and he felt ashamed.

He grabbed the old man and woman and took them outside, saying, 'I am Baron Frederick Von Schubach and have decided to send you to my château in Monaco. I am going to pay for your flights, and you are going to spend a month being waited on hand and foot by my servants. You can use my heated swimming pool, my jacuzzi, my Rolls-Royce and my executive jet, and you'll stay in the Royal suite with the double bed that King Louis the Fourteenth used to own.'

The pensioners were thrilled, and thanked the baron for his kindness.

The tickets arrived and at Newcastle Airport they were handed an envelope each. On looking inside they found £2,000 in cash as spending money, and off they went on the holiday of a lifetime.

The month flew by and the old couple returned to Newcastle Airport. There to meet them was the baron, who took them for a drink.

The old fellow gave him a hearty handshake, saying, 'That was fabulous. We travelled all over Europe in your jet, we drove to the South of France, I've feasted on steaks and champagne and had a whale of a time, but can I ask you one thing?'

The baron nodded and the old man chirped, 'Who's this old woman I've been shacked up with all month?'

*

An old couple from Murton decided that they would go on a second honeymoon to celebrate their 50th wedding anniversary. They had decided to return to the same hotel in Scarborough where they spent their very first night together. So they arrived and were made welcome and shown to the very same room, 20B. The same room, the same bed and very likely the same sheets. 'Do you remember,' said she, 'how you sat on this bed and nibbled my ear?'

'Yes,' said he, 'hang on and I'll just put my teeth in!'

'Do you remember,' said she, 'you were so desperate for me you wouldn't even wait for me to take my stockings off?'

'Yes,' said he, 'but don't panic. Tonight you've got time to knit yersell a pair!'

7

Chat-up lines vary but one of the most basic came from the lad from the City of Sunderland who met a naive girl from Pity Me and asked, 'Do you know the difference between a man's thingy and a chicken leg?'

She said, 'No.'

So he asked, 'Do you want to go on a picnic?'

*

Northern women have traditionally been downtrodden, but they have now redressed the balance and have the ability to firmly trounce their men when necessary. One such lady who returned from the doctor's to find her husband lying as usual on the settee watching football, drinking lager and hoying crisps into his gob.

'Well,' she says, 'that doctor examined me and says that I have a really good body for a woman my age!'

He looks up from the telly and says, 'What about your big fat bum?'

'Oh,' she replied, 'he never mentioned you at all!'

*

Whoever said it was wise to 'get it out in the open' obviously hadn't heard the true story from just outside of Harrogate in 1977. A couple were making love in the back of a Mini when the man slipped his disc. The two were actually stuck together for some time before a passer-by phoned for the police. Two panda cars arrived, plus a fire engine, an ambulance and a WRVS tea van. The only way they could get the couple out was to cut the roof off the Mini. Out came the welding torch and within twenty minutes they pulled the couple, still joined at the cheeky bits, out of the car, separated them and took them off to the hospital.

Wrapped in a sheet they gave the woman a cup of tea and a nurse said, 'Never mind, pet, your husband will be OK.'

The woman started sobbing, saying, 'To hell with him, he's not my husband. But it is my husband's car!'

*

Matty, from Eastfield Dale, Cramlington, asks: 'Did you hear about the woman who was given Valium instead of the birth-control pill? Now she's got fourteen kids and doesn't give a bugger!'

Star Turn

DENISE WELCH

Denise is the North's really big-name actress and star of *Spender*, who has appeared in countless TV and stage roles. Wife of Tim Healey, she is another to have worked with me on the Telethon, when she was persuaded to stand against a wall and let a cowboy hurl knives at her. It was all in a good cause.

It doesn't surprise me that she is *that* good at what she does. She has a rapierlike wit, and a real fun-loving personality. An absolute stunner! Throughout the day she was cracking jokes, as I was, usually at someone's expense! It was a great day, made even better with Denise and Tim's company!

*

Doreen looked lovely in her crimplene frock with lurex bits around the hem, and her boyfriend Donald was taking her for a drive down a lovers' lane.

Donald said, 'You're really dead bonny and beautiful!'

Doreen blushed and said, 'Thank you very much!'

'Your hair is really pretty as well,' added Donald.

Doreen thanked him again.

Donald was on a roll. 'Your eyes are like the deepest blue lagoons!'

Once again Doreen said thanks.

'Your ruby-red lips are beautiful and your teeth shine like pearls!' said Donald, who was laying it on with a trowel.

'Well, what can I say?' said Doreen. 'But can I ask a question?'

'Ask me anything,' answered Donald. 'I would climb the highest mountain for you, swim the widest ocean, anything for you!'

Doreen said, 'Can you drive with one hand?'

Donald's excitement was building. 'Oh yes. Oh yes I can!'

So Doreen replied, 'Well, wipe your nose. It's running!'

*

It was noon on a chilly October day, and out into the pouring rain walked Sammy Morton on his way to the gallows for committing a murder. The rain was lashing down like a monsoon, and Sammy said, 'I'm getting soaked!'

The prison guard said, 'You want to think yourself lucky. I've got to walk back in this!'

ROY KINNEAR

The lovely, cuddly and downright hilarious Roy Kinnear was a guest on my show during his appearances at Newcastle's Theatre Royal in *A Man for All Seasons*, and he was an absolute delight. He talked at length about how he had worked for many

11

years to help the disabled, as his own youngster was that kind of special child. We were totally hypnotised by his sincerity and sharp sense of humour.

I asked him if he had ever been asked to play a romantic lead, instead of a figure of fun.

Roy replied, 'What, with a face like mine? The woman wouldn't reach my lips for my stomach!'

I kept searching for any romantic parts he'd played, and he said this:

'When I was a young actor just starting off, we were doing some role-playing, and we were all supposed to be Eskimos. I played a handsome Eskimo. The director told me to kiss the attractive lady Eskimo. I knew then I'd never take the lead role. I mean how do you get a nose to pucker up?'

*

He was one of the funniest men ever, and I'll never forget him.

FAMOUS NORTHERNERS

SILLY BILLY FLAME, THE COMEDIAN ON BOARD THE TITANIC

Silly Billy had done canny good on the circuit of Northern clubs. He had gone as far as he could, ending up in a mansion house with balls on his gate, a Rolls-Royce in his double garage and a belly that hung over his trousers. Not many Northerners could afford to fill their bellies like that, but Silly Billy had made it to the top, appearing in the regular radio series 'When the Summons Comes In'. He had so much dosh that he wanted to do something else a bit flash, so he decided to book a cruise to America, where the new-fangled movies were being made. Ugly-looking comics like Ben Turpin and Fatty Arbuckle were big stars so he thought he'd stand a chance to become a comic legend too. So he got his agent to book him aboard as the cabaret so the trip would cost him nowt. He was known as being the sort that threw his money around like a man with no arms!

To his credit he was a surprise novelty success, singing songs like 'If You're Proud to be Geet Wealthy Clap Yer Hands!', 'Keep Your Legs

Closed Nelly Hinny' and 'Wherever Ye Gan You're Sure to Leave a Jobby!'

He had refused to sleep in the economy class with the less wealthy; he had to be around the rich. So after some wangling he landed in First Class, using some sponsorship money to cover his room-service bill.

The night of 15 April the ship was off the coast of Newfoundland, and the captain invited all the dignitaries to join him at his table. There were film stars, industrialists, politicians and Silly Billy Flame, suburban superstar. On getting his invitation to dine with the captain Billy ripped it up, saying, 'Ye've got to be kidding. I'm a star, ye cannot expect me to eat wi' the crew!'

The iceberg hit the so-called 'unsinkable' and the ship began to sink.

'Who wanted ice in their drink?' asked Billy.

No one laughed.

'What di ye get if you cross the Atlantic and the *Titanic*?' asked Billy. 'Aboot halfway!'

No one laughed.

'What di ye get if you cross the Atlantic and the *Titanic*?' asked Billy again. 'Wet!' he roared.

Nobody laughed.

The lifeboats were filling up, and life-jackets were being handed out.

'I insist on a Gucci life-jacket!' said Billy. 'I've got balls on my gate and a reputation to live up to!'

Billy was still ploughing away at the passengers as they scurried around looking for escape. 'It may cost hundreds to take a cruise but why is it best to take the *Titanic*?' asked the rotund comic. 'Because it's just a drop in the ocean!'

Nobody laughed!

The ship's band started playing hymns as the last of the lifeboats left. Silly Billy's key to success in the entertainment business had always been: go up, never gan doon. Even so he went down that night . . . but not as well as the band!

MATTY McILHATTON, STOOGE FOR HOUDINI

Harry Houdini was the biggest star of his day, but much of his success he owned to his pal from Peterlee, Matty McIlhatton. It was Matty who had inadvertently created Houdini's most famous stunt: escaping from a water-filled milk churn. Once Matty was walking across the field and stumbled over three milk churns. He thought he had found a cow's nest, so he stole one. After drinking all the milk, he installed it in his outside netty, and after a night on the beer he was sitting on it, doing his business, when he slipped and fell into it – discovering it was almost three-quarters full of stale urine. His cries were overheard by Harry Houdini who rescued him, and it gave him the idea to be an escapologist.

Houdini did a lot of magic tricks once, and set about impressing Matty by pulling fingers out of gloves, hankies out of his nose and Woodbines from his packet.

'Would you be surprised,' asked Harry, 'if I put my hand in your cap and pulled a rabbit out of it?'

Matty said, 'I would, Harry, 'cause I've got my ferret in there!'

Houdini took Matty on a liner where he would

make things disappear. Once he made a man's watch disappear.

Matty shouted, 'It's in your sleeve!'

Houdini made a woman's handbag disappear.

Matty shouted, 'It's tucked down the back of your trousers!'

At that very moment the ship hit some rocks and sank.

Harry and Matty were clinging to a liferaft and bobbing up and down in the North Sea when Matty said, 'I give up! Where's the bloody ship?'

NELLIE GREEN, MARIE STOPES'S FIRST PATIENT

In those dark days before proper contraceptives, Nellie Green had had 52 children. She was only 42 herself. She had had her feet in the stirrups more than John Wayne, and everyone thought she was stork raving mad. She was so very poor even her husband was on HP, so she agreed to be a guinea pig for Marie Stopes who opened the very first Family Planning Clinic in the back of an old van.

Marie Stopes sent Nellie to Amsterdam to try the new Dutch cap. She was away with a Dutchman for a fortnight and returned saying, 'That's nee good, it kept falling off his heed!' She was pregnant again!

After that baby was born, Marie Stopes gave Nellie the coil, which felt like a piece of barbed wire to be placed inside you. Despite having it professionally installed by three Kwikfit fitters, it still didn't work, and soon Nellie was expecting a baby in the spring.

After that child was born, Marie Stopes ordered

her to try the rhythm method. Well, she tried reggae, rap, rave, rock, jazz, classical, folk, country and western, and pop. It made no difference – she still fell pregnant, and let's face it, where are you going to find a band at two o'clock in the morning?

Nellie's family was so large she called her pram 'the blunderbus' and she didn't employ babysitters – she just had a team of sheepdogs! Still, Marie Stopes decided to use Nellie to test the latest gadget, the condom. Two months later Nellie was pregnant again. It seems that the condoms she'd been given were too big for her husband, so she'd cut the ends off.

Marie Stopes was beginning to lose heart, so after Nellie had given birth once more she tried a desperate stroke, giving Nellie a pot of spermicidal cream. The Finnish doctors swore it worked perfectly, and expectations were high. But two months later Nellie was pregnant.

Marie asked what had happened and Nellie replied, 'I couldn't eat it as it was, so I put it on my trifle!'

The midwife was sick to death of Nellie, and was considering fitting swing doors to her womb. Then Marie Stopes suggested the 'withdrawal' method. So off Nellie goes, but two months later she's pregnant again.

'What happened this time?' asked Marie Stopes.

'Well, we took all the money out of both my bank and building society accounts, but it made no difference!'

'You daft woman,' said Marie. 'I meant he had to remove his thingy from you!'

'Well he does that anyway after he's finished,'

17

said Nellie, 'otherwise walking around would be a problem.'

Finally the Pill was invented, and at long last Marie Stopes felt that Nellie was free from the worry of pregnancy. But two months later she was pregnant again.

'Didn't you take the Pill?' barked Marie Stopes.

'I did,' says Nellie, 'every single day. But it kept falling out!'

ERIC OGLETHWAITE, DOG HANDLER TO COMMANDER ROBERT E. PEARY

Leeds man Eric Oglethwaite was with explorer Commander Robert E. Peary when he reached the North Pole in 1909. He was in charge of the huskies, and was almost responsible for the challenge being called off all together. The commander ordered him to delouse the dogs before they set off. So Eric went down to Tesco's and asked the woman for some Omo.

'What d'ye want that for, hinny? It's really strong, mind!' said the shopgirl.

'That's champion,' said Eric, 'it'll dee.' And off he goes.

So that night the commander calls around, and Eric tells him he's got some Omo to wash the dogs.

'Hell's teeth,' says the commander, 'are you sure it'll not hurt them?'

'No bother,' says Eric. 'My brother does his poodle in it every week, and it comes out really white!'

Two days later the commander contacts him again and asks, 'How are the dogs, Eric?'

'I'm sorry, they're all dead,' said Eric.

'I told you,' roared the commander, 'I told you that Omo was really strong, I knew it would kill them!'

'It wasn't the Omo,' said Eric. 'It was putting them through the mangle afterwards that did it!'

BARRY HUNT, THE LOUNGE LIZARD OF LEAM LANE

When it comes to great lovers Barry Hunt was the man. He was renowned as the very best – after all, he had practised a lot on his own. Everyone called him 'Casanova'.

One day when Casanova came home his son looked up at him and said, 'Dad, I want to get married.'

His dad was shocked, saying, 'And who is going to be the lucky lass then?'

'Well, it's going to be Betty Brisket!' said the young lad.

'Not Betty from Widdrington?' said Casanova.

'Aye, that's where she lives!' chirped the boy.

'Ye can't marry her,' said Casanova. 'Ye see, when I was younger I put myself about a bit, and that lass is my daughter, and your sister. You can't marry her!'

Two weeks later the lad came back to his dad, who was playing lighthouses in the bath. 'Dad, I want to get wed!'

'Who is it this time?' said the old Lothario.

'Her name's Madge Davis from North Shields,' replied the boy.

'Ye can't marry her,' said Casanova, 'not if she's Elsie Davis's daughter. I told you how I got about a bit when I was young. She's your sister, and my daughter!'

This happened three more times, and the young lad could take it no more and was sitting on his bed crying. His Mam Tracy came in and asked why he was so upset. The lad explained how five times his father had wrecked his life.

'Take no notice of him,' said his mam, 'he's not your father anyway!'

FRANKIE, NOAH'S BROTHER-IN-LAW

The Ark was finally built, it was bucketing down, and Noah was getting them on board: two dogs, two cats, two horses, two cows, one girl from the *Sunday Sport*, when Noah's brother-in-law said, 'Howay Noah, do you really think it's wise to set sail during the elephants' mating season?'

'Nee bother Frankie. It's got to be now, God's sending the flood.'

'I think it's patter, Noah,' said Frankie. 'I'm getting off. I believe in God and if he really exists he'll save me!'

So the Ark sails away after narrowly avoiding the Animal Liberationists, who would have set all the animals free.

Frankie stood alone with water up to his knees, and rising all the time.

At that moment a rowing boat arrived and the

local Rabbi said, 'Howay in Frankie, you'll ruin your Doctor Martens!'

'Hadaway,' said Frankie. 'I believe in God, he'll save me!'

Twenty minutes later the water was lapping around his chest and a canoe appeared with Zaffa, the Asian lad from the Cash and Carry, in it.

'Howay in Frankie,' he said. 'If we're swift we can sink a few tonight!'

'No hadaway,' said Frankie. 'God will save me, I'm not worried!'

So Zaffa paddled off and by this time the water was up to Frankie's chin.

Then a spaceship zoomed overhead, and hovered inches above the surface of the water. The door opened with a buzz, and a strange alien creature shouted, 'Woah Frankie, get in man, ye'll drooned doon there!'

'Get stuffed,' yelled Frankie. 'God will save me!'

So the alien sped off, and within minutes Frankie had drowned.

He gets up to Heaven and storms into God's office, and says, 'I want a word with you, Mush!'

'Aye,' says God. 'What's up, son?'

'You sent that flood, didn't ye?' said Frankie.

'Yes hinny,' said God. 'I couldn't help it, my pipes burst, and this is Heaven so there's no plumbers up here!'

'Well, I put my faith in you to protect me,' said Frankie, 'and what did you do? You let me drown. So thanks a lot!'

God says, 'Divvn't blame me, I sent two boats and a spaceship!'

DR HINDU BARNARD, THE FIRST-EVER TRANSPLANT SURGEON

Hindu Barnard was born in a small house on Sydney Grove in Newcastle and after reading the book *Frankenstein* he began the first-ever transplants. He tried the first hair transplant, but his patient looked stupid with a kidney on his head, and the scandal forced the young doctor to hide in the Scottish Border country.

One day he came upon a man with a major belly ache, rolling around the ground in severe pain. The local Scottish doctor had examined him, checked him for appendix, stomach chills, bad diet, and wind – all to no avail.

'Help me,' yelled the man, and Dr Hindu waded in.

'I am sorry to say,' said Dr Hindu, 'but your belly is knackered. You need a stomach transplant.'

'Impossible,' said the doctor. 'Where will you get a donor from? No, he'll not survive.'

Dr Hindu was not put off by this and said, 'We are so far from the nearest hospital I'll have to operate here!' So in the absence of a human donor, he took the stomach from a cow, and transplanted it into the man's tum.

Almost at once the man was feeling better; the operation was a total and complete triumph. Word spread back to Newcastle and Dr Hindu Barnard returned as a hero, a pathfinder and obviously Britain's finest surgeon!

The general hospital examined the patient, and gave him the all-clear. As he came out, the man was interviewed by the newspapers, who asked how he was.

'It was a first-class job. I feel smashing, I'm perfectly fit. Not only that, but I'm expecting a calf in October!'

Star Turn

FREDDIE MERCURY

When I first got into the entertainment business I was a fan of a new up-and-coming band called Queen. They had made only one album, simply called *Queen*, and from there they soared to an international rock supergroup.

What seemed like a lifetime later I was asked to appear at St James's Park with them to set up the show. I was happy to do so, and as was the norm, I approached the record company for an interview, ideally with Freddie Mercury. I'd met and inter-viewed Brian May, the guitarist, who then had hair like a burst couch, and I wanted to get Freddie this time. The record company did their best but came up empty. I decided to take matters into my own hands, and took a mobile recorder to the stadium to sort it out myself. I had a pass so getting in and setting up what I was planning to do took barely half an hour, giving me time to find out where the band were staying.

Off I went and saw a batch of chunky security personnel escorting the group into a car, despite the attentions of around forty fans. I walked into the hotel and asked the receptionist about the band, and as I was doing so, I couldn't believe my eyes when I saw Freddie Mercury and a crew member walking into the restaurant. I walked towards the door and shouted, 'Excuse me Freddie, but I'm hosting your show this afternoon. Any chance of a word?'

He stopped, turned around and said, 'I've got to eat now, and then I've got to go to the stadium.'

'Just a quick word?' said I, and he said with a wide grin, 'All right. Just a quick word, at the stadium though!'

I'd done it! Off I went to St James's Park and bided my time. I was there when the band arrived during one of the support bands. I had done my thing and was free to concentrate on getting as much down on tape as possible. Freddie was led into specially adapted units behind the stage, and I was stopped from getting there by burly Cockney security men.

Then Queen were about to go on, and the band had to pass me, so I thought, right, I'm going to prick your conscience for not giving me the interview. So I stood there and as he went past he said to a man with a walkie-talkie, 'I'm going to have a quick word with him after the show, OK?' The man agreed, we exchanged a respectful nod, and off he went to perform one of the greatest live shows the North East had ever seen!

Patience was never a great virtue of mine, yet I had trailed this man all day. When the show ended the band came off, totally soaked with sweat, and I was still there. The band were to be moved out of the stadium at once, before the capacity crowd flooded the streets. With a towel around his shoulders Freddie was ushered towards me. My tape machine was ready and I knew exactly what I wanted to ask him.

He walked straight past me and I shouted, 'What about my quick word?'

Freddie smiled and shouted, 'OK then. "Goodbye"!'

JOE CAFFREY

One of the North's finest actors and star of many local and national shows including *Byker Grove* and the movie *Love in Tropical Places* with Alison Doody. Arguably the North's best leading man, he's worked with me in three pantos, once sharing the lead role with his best pal Robson Green, star of *Casualty* and *Soldier Soldier*. The North is awash with this high standard of acting talent, as Joe's actors' cooperative Bridge Management Services will testify. His joke is a Northern classic:

A man ran into his local barber's and asked if he could have his hair cut straight away.

The barber said, 'Hadaway man, the shop's chockablock full, there's a queue ye knaa!'

The man said, 'But it's vital I get my hair cut, I'm flying down to London in an hour!'

The barber said, 'That's nowt to do with me, bonny lad. Ye'll take your turn or stay hairy!'

'But I'm going to see the Queen at Buckingham Palace, man, this isn't a job interview or a holiday!' said the man.

Well, the old barber's mouth just fell open and

he said, 'So what are ye doing with her Majesty, like?'

'Well,' said the bloke, 'I'm getting presented with a medal for my length of employment in the Civil Service!'

The barber twigged he was sincere, so he asked all the customers if they minded him jumping the queue, as this was a very special reason.

His hair was done, off the bloke raced to the airport.

One week later the man popped back into the barber's.

The barber said, 'Why it's yee isn't it, the lad what went doon ti the Palace!'

'Aye,' said the man.

'And there's your medal,' said the barber. 'Did she pin that on you?'

'She did,' said the man.

The barber couldn't believe that the Queen had actually touched that very lapel. He asked, 'Did she say owt to you?'

'She did that,' said the man. 'When she pinned the medal on she leaned over and spoke to me!'

'What did she say?' asked the barber.

The man replied, 'Well, she said, "Who the hell cut your hair like that?" '

DEBBIE WILSON

Debbie is a terrific dancer from Northumberland, having led troupes on tour in Hong Kong, Singapore and Greece. Denny spotted her working at an Old Music Hall at the Maltings in Berwick, and tipped me the wink. She is absolutely gorgeous and

27

has a tremendous personality, so I decided to give her a break in panto, specially writing a part for her as 'Shakira', an Egyptian princess. She deserves to get on in the business, she's a good friend and now can add 'actress' to her list of credits.

A man went to a pet shop with Percy his pet canary and demanded his money back.

The pet-shop owner asked him what was wrong.

'This canary has only got one leg!' said the bloke.

The owner nodded, saying, 'I know that.'

The bloke was really angry, saying, 'If you knew that why sell me a one-legged bird?'

'Listen,' said the pet-shop owner, 'you told me you wanted a bird that was the best singer. This bird is the best singer I've got. If you wanted a dancer you should have said so!'

GANNIN' DOON THE DOCTOR'S

A Macam (chap from Sunderland) visits his doctor and says, 'Doctor, you've got to help me. Last night I was doing my party trick by putting my glass eye in my pint of lager, when I accidentally took a swig and swallowed it. I've been in the netty (toilet) with my fishing net all week, but it just won't come out. I think it's stuck up there!'

So the doctor says, 'Go on then, drop your kegs (trousers) and bend over and I'll have a look up your bum.'

So this the Wearsider does and the doctor is staring at his backside saying, 'I'm really sorry, I don't see it!'

The Macam says, 'That's funny, because I can see you!'

*

Bella from Byker was asked by the Family Planning Clinic to take a sample in, but they didn't expect a full galvanised bucket!

*

Frankie Brown wasn't 'heducated' very well; he only went to school for one day, and didn't learn anything – it was a night school. So when his wife

29

asked him to go and get a parsnip, he was away three days and came back with a vasectomy.

*

What's a spot's favourite pop group?
Squeeze.
What's the best room for breeding spots?
The Zitting Room.
What do you call a spot in wellies?
Puss in Boots.
What did the spot say when he saw his pal crying?
What's the matter?

*

Eddie from Shiney Row needed help because he couldn't sleep, so the doctor asked him why.
'It's my sister,' said Eddie, 'she thinks she's a fridge!'
'Why, is that a problem?' enquired the doctor.
Eddie replied, 'She sleeps with her mouth open and that little light keeps me awake!'

*

My mate Denny borrowed £4,000 to get some plastic surgery. I'll never get the money back, because now I don't know what he looks like!

*

Bob from Cramlington burst into the surgery at the health centre and said, 'Doctor, I think I'm going mad, I just love fresh cream doughnuts!' The doctor grinned, saying, 'Don't be silly, Bob, there's nothing wrong with that, I'm partial to them myself!'
Bob replied, 'Really? Sexy little devils aren't they!'

*

In these days of fighting pollution, I was careful to

buy some air freshener without CFCs and I read the can. It said: 'Bring the clean natural freshness of a country meadow indoors. Freshens the air in your home with a clean back-to-nature scent. As refreshing as the summer grass and fragrant flowers of the countryside. WARNING: Inhaling the contents of this can may be harmful or fatal!'

*

Is it true that you can cure 'pins and needles' by acupuncture?

*

The hospitals in the North East pride themselves on being the best transplanters in the business. Yet after one amazing success story of a man who had a heart and lung transplant, a joke zoomed around the clubs.

What's the worst thing about having a heart and lung transplant?

Coughing up someone else's phlegm!

*

What do you get if you cross a food mixer and a nymphomaniac with a lisp?

A girl who'll whisk anything!

*

Mary from Fenham was showing a Yank around Newcastle, and was truly sick of the American's boasting and bragging. According to him everything in America was bigger, better, cleaner etc.

So when they reached Grey's Monument the American asked what it was. Mary replied, 'That's Earl Grey's statue.'

The American then asked what he'd died of.

'Gall stones,' answered Mary. 'That's one of them that he's standing on!'

A book worth getting hold of: *Alternative Contraception* by Mr Completely.

*

Geordie Hall from Slatyford went to his doctor and, after a lengthy examination, asked what was wrong with him.

The doctor said, 'Well, you're fat, you drink too much, you're dirty, smelly and basically a lazy and idle pig!'

'I knaa that,' said Geordie, 'but can you give it a Latin name so I can have a sick note for work?'

*

Poor little Ellen had no bust at all and was rather plain, and she married a plain bloke from Whickham. He had a few quid and sent her off to a plastic surgeon for some breast enlargements. Two months later she returned looking tremendous. They divorced soon after. Apparently there was a big bust-up between them!

*

In the corridors of Newcastle General Hospital two African doctors were having a heated conversation.

'No it's not,' shouted one, 'it's WOOOMBA, W-O-O-O-M-B-A, WOOMBA!'

'You're wrong,' said the other doctor, 'it's definitely WUMBA! W-U-M-B-A!'

This went on for quite some time until a nursing sister quietened them down and said, 'Listen, you're both wrong. In Britain it's called womb. W-O-M-B, womb!'

Then she walked away leaving the two doctors looking very puzzled.

'What is she talking about?' said the first doctor.

'I bet she's never even seen a hippopotamus, let alone heard one break wind underwater!'

*

How do you get rid of unwanted pubic hair?
  Spit it out!

*

My mate Denny was a premature baby – his dad wasn't expecting him.

*

Innocence is asking three of your friends to join in with foreplay.

*

During a sporting event at Gateshead International Stadium a man tried to grab American runner Florence Griffith Joyner, better known as Flo Jo.
  He told police he only wanted to try out his new pacemaker!

*

Woody from Bedlington goes into his doctor and says, 'You've got to help me Doc, I think I'm a dog!'
  'How long have you felt this way?' asked the doctor.
  'Ever since I was a puppy!' replied Woody.
  The doctor asked him to take a seat but Woody refused. 'I'm not allowed on the furniture!'

*

In the early 1980s I was invited to the 100th birthday of a Newcastle man, at Brunswick Methodist Church, behind Fenwick's in the heart of the city. He was surrounded by about thirty women, all in their 80s and 90s.
  I asked the old fellow how he was going to celebrate his birthday.

33

He chuckled, saying, 'Well, I'm going to have a Guinness and then make love to one of these!'

Everybody laughed: 'The Queen sent him a telegram, Prince Philip sent him a diagram!'

*

Alfie Robinson woke up in Shotley Bridge Hospital on his 100th birthday, and looked at his naked body. 'Hands,' said he, 'you're one hundred years old today!' Then he looked down at his legs and said, 'Legs, you are one hundred years old today!'

Then he looked down at the wee willy winkie that was once his manhood and said, 'Well mate, if you had lived you'd have been one hundred years old today!'

*

I once visited Ashington General Hospital because I'd come out in a rash all over my body. So they asked me to go into a cubicle and take all of my clothes off and put on one of those little robes that leave your bum waving in the breeze. I had sat there for nearly an hour when three women in white coats came in, one carrying a clipboard. They whispered to each other then one walked up to me, lifted the bottom of my gown, and looked straight at my cheeky bits.

She returned to her two friends, then another woman strode towards me, lifted up the hem of my gown and once again perused my vitals.

Well, I was sick of this, so I grabbed the bottom of my gown and lifted it off, right over my head.

'All right, now you can see everything,' I yelled. 'What do you think?'

'Very nice,' said one of the three.

'That's not what I meant,' I explained. 'What do you think is wrong?'

The ladies shook their heads. 'How do you expect us to know? We're the cleaners!'

*

My mate Denny's wife has gone into hospital for plastic surgery. She's having her credit cards removed.

*

Why do women rub their eyes in the morning?

They've got nothing else to scratch!

*

There was a family of cauliflowers – Daddy Collie, Mammy Collie and Baby Collie. One day Baby Collie was playing in the garden when he fell off his moontain bike. He was rushed to hospital and he was hurried into intensive care. After waiting for hours agonising over what was to become of her son, Mammy Collie asked the doctor, 'Is he going to be all right?'

The doctor shook his head, 'I'm sorry Mrs Collie, but he'll be a vegetable for the rest of his life!'

*

A bloke went into a trendy Jesmond clinic for a vasectomy, but the doctor had been on the gin and accidentally cut off one of his testicles. Fortunately the doctor knew he had a spare in a jar in his study, so he sent a nurse to get it. As she ran along the corridor from his office she tripped and the testicle rolled across the floor and one of the porters squashed it flat. In a blind panic the nurse searched for something else that could replace it. The only thing of similar size and shape that she could find was a pickled onion, so she grabbed one from the canteen and zoomed back to the operating theatre.

The vasectomy was finished off, and the man sent home with explicit instructions to return in a fort-night.

Two weeks flew by and the man visited the sur-geon who asked, 'Well, Mr Squire, any problems?'

'None at all, doctor,' said the patient. 'Every-thing's fine, but could you tell me one thing?'

The doctor nodded.

'Why is it that whenever I see a cheese sandwich I get an erection?'

*

A bloke from Stockton has serious BO and his doctor recommended that he get a coconut, scoop out the insides and rub the milk and sap all over his armpits, and then rub milk chocolate on the top.

'Doctor you were right,' said the lad. 'It got rid of my body odour, but it does smell of coconut!'

The doctor said, 'It's bounty!'

*

Everyone knows that halitosis is better than no breath at all, but Davy from Seaham had had enough. He was sick of people commenting on it, so he visited a country doctor who believed in herbal cures.

The doctor took one whiff of his tainted breath and said, 'I suggest you go out in the fields first thing in the morning. Once there find a fresh, hot and steamy cowpat, and chew it for twenty-five minutes.'

Davy said, 'Will that cure me, doctor?'

'No,' answered the GP, 'but it will take the edge off it!'

*

A very butch-looking lady had been trying to win a place in Britain's Olympic squad for the javelin and the shot, and she returned to her doctor to complain about her hormone-replacement tablets.

'What's the matter with them?' asked the doctor.

The woman shyly replied, 'It's just that I'm starting to grow a lot of body hair.'

'Yes, I can see a little on your chest,' said the doctor. 'How far down does it go?'

The girl replied, 'All the way down to my testicles!'

*

'Doctor, doctor, I feel like a sideboard!'

The doctor shook his head, saying, 'How's your chest then?'

The man replied, 'I said a sideboard, not a full wall unit!'

*

Harry from Hexham ran into his doctor's surgery and said, 'Doctor, you'll never believe this, but my willy is turning into a flower!'

The doctor replied, 'Poppycock!'

*

Two neighbours were chatting and one said, 'I'm sure that breakfast-show DJ has had his face lifted.'

'What makes you think that?' asked her friend.

She replied, 'It's as plain as the nose on his forehead!'

*

Basil from Greenside went into the chemist and asked for a packet of condoms half an inch long.

The assistant told him, 'Half an inch long, that would only fit a mouse!'

'I know,' said Basil. 'The house is overrun with them.'

*

My mate Denny paid £4,000 for a sex change and what's he got to show for it? Not a sausage!

*

Did you hear about the nugget from Harrogate who put his teeth in back to front and ate himself?

*

A man dashed into his doctor's office and shouted, 'You've got to help me doctor, I'm shrinking. Two days ago I was 6'8" and today I'm only 2'6".'

The doctor said, 'Well, you'll just have to be a little patient!'

*

They closed a health-food shop in Newcastle when they discovered that their organic dental floss was in fact pubic hair!

*

My mate Denny is so ugly that if he left his body to medical science, the hospital would contest the will.

*

What is bright red and stupid?

A blood clot!

*

Vasectomy means never having to say you're sorry!

*

Little Terry met this bonny girl called Tracy on a floating nightclub and after a few weeks of courting he had persuaded her to go on the Pill. Their sex life was great, and she started saying that she wanted to stop taking the Pill. Terry, being a dope, was frightened of using condoms and asked her why.

Tracy said, 'Well you told me it would improve my hearing, well it doesn't. Anyway it falls out of my ear when I'm dancing!'

*

Walter from Berwick was a bit naive about sex so he visited the Family Planning Clinic and asked about condoms. The woman told him all about them and said, 'So Walter, if you'd like a box of condoms it will cost you a pound plus tax.'

Walter says, 'Divven't bother aboot the tacks, I'll tie them on!'

*

A husband was being dragged around the Metrocentre, Europe's biggest shopping centre, on the outskirts of Gateshead, by a very loud and belligerent wife. 'You don't deserve me,' she said.

He thought for a bit then chirped, 'I don't deserve piles either but I've got them!'

*

A doctor was reaching into his inside pocket and started trying to write up one of his reports with a rectal thermometer. 'Bugger,' he said, 'some bum's got my pen!'

*

My very first live guest appearance after getting a job on radio was at a very exclusive nudist camp, north of Wooler in Northumberland. One of the girls from there visited a local GP and asked for him to examine her. After various tests he proclaimed, 'Well, I can tell you quite positively that you are pregnant!'

She was instantly angered, barking, 'That's where you're wrong, for I am a naturist, we only make love to one another with our eyes!'

The doctor said, 'Well, it appears one of your friends is cockeyed!'

*

A lass from Galashiels spent twenty minutes walking up and down the street before she summoned up the courage to go into her dentist's. Once inside she visited the toilet twice, got the shakes and almost burst into tears when the receptionist asked for her to go through. The dentist was aware of how scared she was and tried to reassure her.

'You know,' she said, 'I'd rather have a baby than a filling!'

The dentist said, 'Howay, pet, make your mind up. I've got to adjust the chair!'

*

If I was going to be a doctor I'd be tempted by private practice. Can you imagine a better job than getting women to take all their clothes off then sending their husband the bill?

*

A lass from Cowpen visited her doctor with stomach pains and after various tests the doctor told her that she was pregnant.

'If I were you I'd go home and tell your husband,' suggested the GP.

'I haven't got a husband,' barked the lass.

'Well, go home and tell your lover then,' he added.

Surly as owt she said, 'I haven't got a lover, nor have I had one, so now what should I do then?'

The doctor thought for a moment then said, 'Well, I'd go back home to Cowpen and watch out of your window tonight for a star appearing in the East!'

My mate Denny went into hospital because one of his testicles swelled up like a beach ball. The doctor prepared some anaesthetic, and walked towards him with this large needle.

Denny backed into a corner so the doctor said, 'Don't worry, Mr Ferguson – it's just a little prick with a needle.'

Denny said, 'I know you are!'

*

The North East leads the world in spare-part surgery, providing patients all over the world with organs for transplant. Basil Hunter from Blaydon was involved in a road accident and lost his right hand. Within minutes the spare-part surgery team was trawling hospitals for a replacement right hand. Sadly they didn't have any men's hands, only a woman's, but it would have to do and after hours of microsurgery it was duly attached.

Two weeks later Basil returned to the hospital and the doctor asked if he'd had any problems with it.

Basil shook his head. 'No, doctor, it's been very canny. It can hold me knife and fork. It can pick up me chips, hold me pint pot and even play my accordion. The only problem is when I go to the toilet it won't let go!'

*

I visit all the hospitals around the North just about every Christmas, and I came across this bloke in bed saying, 'I hope I'm sick, I hope I'm sick!'

I asked him why he wished he was sick and he replied, ''Cos I'd hate to be well and feel like this!'

*

In one of the North's private clinics a nurse asked the doctor, 'What are we operating on this bloke for?'

The doctor said, 'Two thousand pounds!'

'You don't catch my drift, doctor,' she replied. 'I mean what has he got?'

The doctor repeated, 'Two thousand pounds!'

*

Young doctors are very badly paid, and one got so desperate he ran into a bank wearing his surgical mask, and pretending to have a gun, handed a note across the counter to the cashier. She couldn't read it!

*

My mate Denny went into his doctor's surgery with tiny pink spots all over his body.

The doctor asked, 'Denny, have you ever had this before?'

Denny nodded and the doctor said, 'Well, you've got it again!'

*

The airline doctor was examining a pilot well into his fifties and asked, 'When did you last have sex?'

The pilot thought for a while and said 'Around 1955.'

The doctor was stunned. 'So very long ago?'

'What do you mean, long ago?' chirped the pilot. 'It's only 21.15 now!'

*

Do doctors who treat people with amnesia ask them to pay in advance?

*

Barry Douglas is now called Caroline after an accidental sex change at a hospital on Teeside.

He went in to get his tonsils out, but they wheeled the trolley into the operating theatre the wrong way round!

*

Old Jeannie from Backworth went into the doctor's and shouted, 'Doctor, Doctor, I've forgotten to take my contradictive pill!'

The doctor said, 'Madam, you're ignorant!'

She said, 'I know – three months!'

*

Now Jackie, one of the wide lads from Benwell, was a bit thick, and after years of sitting on cold walls he had acquired the worst case of haemorrhoids you've ever seen – a bunch of grapes that even the man from Del Monte wouldn't say yes to. Finally he went to his doctor's and owned up to the problem. The doctor prescribed some powerful suppositories, pain-killers and a soft cushion.

A fortnight later Jackie was back and the doctor asked whether the suppositories had worked.

'Worked?' said Jackie. 'Not at all. They tasted horrible as well. I might as well have shoved them up my arse!'

*

A young lass burst out of her doctor's surgery sobbing her heart out, so I pulled him aside and said, 'What did you do to upset that lass?'

The doctor said, 'I merely told her she was pregnant when she wasn't.'

I said, 'What a cruel thing to do, why did you?'

The doctor replied, 'Well, it cured her hiccups didn't it?'

*

A bloke went into a private clinic, and they told

him he only had six months to live. After five months and three weeks he told them that he couldn't afford the bill, so they gave him another six months.

*

Did you hear about the man from Darlington who took Andrews' Liver Salts twice a day for over seventy years? He died a month ago and last Thursday they had to send people up to the cemetery and beat his liver to death with a stick!

*

Even Prince Charles seems keen on alternative medicine these days, but it's never more alternative than in Northumberland. Auld Meg from Alnwick has provided bizarre cures for over thirty years. One day a young girl called Karen visited her because she was very embarrassed about her tiny bust measurement, and begged Auld Meg to help her.

Meg told her to repeat a rhyme, and her breasts would grow.

So for six months everywhere Karen went she repeated, 'I must, I must, I must increase my bust!' Over and over again she would say it, and slowly but surely her bust began to grow.

During a trip to London she was repeating the rhyme as usual when a Geordie voice called out, 'Who ye, ye gan to Auld Meg in Alnwick, divven't ye?'

The girl blushed and said, 'Yes I do, but how do you know?'

The bloke walked away saying, 'Hickory dickory dock . . .'

Star Turn

SAMMY JOHNSON

Sammy is one of the North's greatest actors, currently revelling in the success of TV's *Spender*, where he plays Stick, Jimmy Nail's dodgy pal. He is a man I very nearly worked with, and I regret missing out on the experience.

He sent this doozie of a joke:

The brothers Fut from Wallsend were lying in bed one night, when brother Fut woke up brother Fut Fut and said, 'Fut Fut, I don't feel very well!' So Fut Fut woke up Fut Fut Fut, and said, 'Fut Fut Fut, Fut doesn't feel very well!'

So off they all go to the doctor's, and Fut was given some medicine. Well, later that night after several swigs of the medicine, sadly Fut died.

Two days later at a quiet funeral in Tynemouth, Fut was buried.

The following night Fut Fut woke up Fut Fut Fut, and said, 'Fut Fut Fut, I'm not feeling very well!'

So Fut Fut Fut called in the doctor who produced a bottle of the same medicine that he had prescribed earlier.

Fut Fut Fut said, 'Hang on, that's the medicine that you gave Fut. Now you're giving it to Fut Fut. Come on, we've already got one Fut in the grave!'

TERRY JOYCE

Having worked as a comedian on the Northern club circuit I can testify how tough a life it is. Yet comic Terry Joyce has built up a reputation as being one of the best of the best. He's come up with a variety of great Northern stories.

I visited the doctor's and asked him to give me a full medical, and he says, 'I'm sorry Terry, I can't find a single thing wrong with you. It must be the drink!'

I replied, 'It's all right Doctor, I'll come back when you're sober!'

*

I went back a couple of weeks later to see my doctor and had another medical.

'I'm sorry to tell you this Terry, but you'll never work again,' said the doctor.

I asked him why and he replied, 'Because you're a lazy bastard!'

*

I told my doctor that I had insomnia and asked him what I needed. He replied, 'A good night's sleep!'

*

There's two donkeys in a rowing boat on Saltwell Park. The first donkey says, 'Ee-oar!'

The second donkey says, 'Hadaway I'm tired, ye-oar!'

WHAT WE'VE THUNK!

In the old TV series *Kung Fu*, star David Carradine said, 'It is not enough to know the answers, better to understand the questions.' So here is a batch of those kind of things!

Why don't toilets on aeroplanes have frosted glass? Who's going to peep in there at 25,000 feet?
*
It's a small world but I wouldn't like to paint it.
*
You never know how dirty your hands are until you peel a hard-boiled egg!
*
You never know how deep a puddle is until you're standing in it!
*
Bald burglars have more hair than brains.
*
If a bucket of fog was stolen would it be mist?
*
There are two sides to every question, the wrong side and our side!
*
Praise is that by which someone convinces you of

something about yourself that you had always suspected.

*

When money burns your pocket you'll not be alone at the fire!

*

What is the definition of fear?

Being stuck in a two-mile-long traffic jam at the Tyne Tunnel when you realise you've just had three glasses of orange juice, two cups of coffee and a bran muffin!

*

Sex is like mathematics – add bed, take away clothes, divide legs and multiply!

*

Is it true that if you cross an octopus and a bale of straw you get a broom with eight handles?

*

Is it true that if you cross a motorway on a mountain bike you get run over?

*

RECIPE FOR LOVE CAKE
Two ounces of teasing
Two ounces of squeezing
Two ounces of ruby-red lips
All mixed together in a young man's arms in a dark corner.

*

HEADLINE NEWS

The following samples were culled from local newspapers, and are proof positive that there are more than a fair share of editors with a sense of humour

– or, more likely, they didn't spot them until it was too late!

'MAGISTRATES MAY ACT ON INDECENT SHOWS'

'LOCAL BOBBY FINDS DEAD BODY IN CEMETERY'

'THE AUDIENCE TRIED TO SPOIL THE PLAY, BUT THE ACTORS SUCCEEDED'

'TWO BUSINESS LADIES REQUIRE SLEEPING PARTNER'

'STERILITY MAY BE HEREDITARY'

'DEEP-FREEZE MEAT, THE BEST SCOTTISH BEEF FROM WALES'

*

LAST WORDS THAT ARE FAMOUSLY COMMON

'Don't worry, of course I've got right of way!'

'Over my dead body.'

'Don't worry, it's harmless!'

'Yes, I'm sure I switched it off!'

'Watch this for acceleration!'

'You wouldn't dare!'

'Oh yeah, you and whose army?'

'This really corners well!'

*

FAMOUS PROVERBS NO ONE KNOWS

A man who has never travelled doesn't know what it's like to travel.

When it's all said and done, it's all said and done.

If I were you I wouldn't be me.

If at first you don't succeed, that's about normal.

A nod's as good as a wink to a dyslexic self-abuser!

You can lead a horse to water but you have to drag it to the knacker's yard.

Never leave till tomorrow what you can do today. Because if you do it today and you like it, you can do it again tomorrow!

It's an ill wind that clears the bar.

You can tell a girl who is a real brick – she's always ready to be laid!

In a nudist household, who wears the trousers?

When the man who invented the drawing board got it wrong, what did he go back to?

*

If banks make so much money why do they keep their pens on chains?

Everybody with any knowledge of football knows that Brian Clough should have been England Manager had the Football Association not been cowardly. An example of his talent took place when Newcastle United were playing away at Nottingham Forest one cold and dreary Wednesday evening in November.

It was an exciting match, balanced on a knife edge, when the floodlights failed and everyone was plunged into blackness.

The Forest electrician was sent for, and he worked on the circuit board to no avail. He beavered away with the back-up generator but couldn't get it to kick into life. On hearing this Brian Clough was furious, grabbed a loud-hailer and walked into the centre of the pitch. 'Now listen everybody,' boomed that distinctive voice. 'I want you all to raise your hands above your head and start clapping.'

At that moment everyone began with thunderous applause, because if you don't do what Brian says he's been known to give people a slapping.

The clapping worked, and within seconds all of the floodlights exploded into life, smothering the pitch with light.

The electrician was gobsmacked and as Brian walked off the pitch he said, 'Mr Clough, how did you do that? The circuit board is blown!'

Brian smiled wryly and replied, 'Hasn't anybody ever told you? "Many hands make light work!" '

*

I was once reading one of these books of amazing facts and I looked up at my mate Denny and said,

'Do you know that every time I breathe a man dies?'

'Really?' said Denny. 'Have you tried changing your toothpaste?'

*

THE LEAST COMFORTING NEWS YOU'VE EVER BEEN GIVEN

'Good news, it's only your wisdom teeth that have to come out!'

'He's alive . . . well, what's left of him!'

'We know where your stolen car is. If you want it back bring a fire extinguisher!'

'The rash will subside within a year or two.'

'Your exhaust will be fitted within an hour. We spotted a few other things too!'

'Darling, I've got trouble with the car, but don't worry – I think I've flooded the engine. The crane is winching it out of the river now!'

'We've found your goldfish, it was in next door's cat!'

'Darling, I won't ever argue with you again . . . I'm leaving.'

*

There are few things more frightening than a feminist teacher with no sense of humour. Well Ms Steiner was such a woman.

One day she was taking a class and decided on a role-playing game to see if the pupils could recognise everyday objects. The idea was to allow them the opportunity to be descriptive.

She said, 'Right, now I'm holding something in my hand. It's round, small and yellow. What do you think it is?'

Little Matty shot his hand up in the air. Ms Steiner knew that Matty always gave the most disgusting replies, so she ignored him and asked little Lisa in the front, who said, 'Is it a grapefruit?'

Ms Steiner said, 'No, Lisa, it is a lemon, but it shows that you were thinking!'

The teacher then picked up another object and said, 'Now I've got something in my hand, it's small and round and red. What is it?'

Once again it was Matty who had his hand in the air first and Ms Steiner said, 'Matty, I'm not picking you, because you always give stupid and dirty answers. Martin, what do you think it is?'

Martin said, 'Is it an apple?'

'No,' answered the teacher, 'actually it's a cherry, but it shows you're thinking!'

At this Matty stuck his hand in the air again and Ms Steiner fired him a cynical glance then asked, 'What is it, Matty?'

Grinning, Matty replied, 'Ms Steiner, I have something in my hand, it's about one and a half inches long, it's thin with a red tip. What is it?'

Ms Steiner blushed a deep red, shuddered involuntarily with rage and yelled, 'How dare you? Get out here right now and stand in the corner!'

Matty got up and walked to the corner and looked

at the class, saying, 'Actually it was a matchstick but it shows she was thinking!'

*

Schoolrooms are the places where we learn our first mind games. One day a beautiful schoolteacher arrived to take a class full of boys. This girl was gorgeous and wore a short skirt that started riding up as soon as she sat at her desk. As the class worked on their project she spotted a boy leaning over looking at her legs. 'Hey, you,' she shouted, 'what have you been looking at?'

The boy was embarrassed but answered, 'Miss, I'm sorry, but I saw your stocking top!'

The teacher replied, 'Pack up your books and get to the Head of Year. I'm suspending you for the rest of today, and sending a note home to your parents.'

A few moments later her skirt had ridden up a little higher and another boy was leaning at an angle of 45 degrees and she yelled, 'And what are you looking at?'

The lad nearly fell off his seat, then replied, 'I'm sorry miss, I couldn't take my eyes off your frilly French knickers!'

'Pack up your books,' said the student teacher, 'and off you go to the headmaster. I am suspending you for a month and then I'm ringing your mam and dad.'

Her skirt kept riding up as the project continued, and it was then that little Maurice dropped his ruler. As he bent down to pick it up he couldn't fail to notice what everyone was aware of.

Before the teacher could call his name Maurice

stood up, pushed his books into his haversack and started walking towards the door.

'Where are you going?' enquired the teacher.

Maurice replied, 'After what I've just seen my school days are over!'

THE HOOSE AND RELATED DISASTERS

Three housewives, Tracy, Sharon and Sarah, were sitting around the kitchen table talking about their children.

'I called my son Patrick because he was born on St Patrick's Day,' said Tracy.

'Eeh, that's peculiar,' said Sharon. 'I called my lad George because he was born on St George's Day!'

'Getaway,' said Tracy.

At this Sarah looked up at the clock and said, 'I'm sorry girls, I must go, our Pancake will be home from school any minute!'

*

Elsie was in the kitchen when her husband Willie came in and placed a brand new video recorder on the kitchen table. 'There you are, darlin',' said Willie, 'I know you've always wanted one so I've been and bought one!'

She was thrilled, but then stopped, saying, 'How can you afford it?'

Willie replied, 'Easy. I got it in part exchange for our telly!'

*

What does a Northern woman do with her bum every morning?

Send him to work.

*

When I was sixteen my mam asked me what I'd like for my birthday, so I told her: 'I'd like a torch so that I can go courting!'

My mam says, 'Divvn't be stupid, I didn't need a torch when I was courting!'

I says, 'Yes, but look what you ended up with!'

*

Jackie and John are sitting in the pub and Jackie says, 'I got rid of 200 pounds of ugly fat last week!'

'Blimey, how did you manage that?' asks John.

Jackie replies, 'I got a divorce!'

*

Keith had to get a divorce because his wife insisted that he keep her pet goat in the bedroom with them. The smell was driving him crazy and he applied for his *decree nisi*. When I asked him why he couldn't open a window, Keith replied: 'What, and let my pigeons out?'

*

I told my mate Denny that his wife had wonderfully thin lips. He said, 'It's not surprising, the amount of exercise they get!'

*

Sex is like a snow storm. You never know how much you are going to get or how long it will last!

*

Mary said, 'I'm not saying my husband is fat, but when I iron his knickers I go on a sponsored walk!'

*

A Bigg Market girl was being consoled by her friend

after her divorce. 'I don't know what went wrong, we once had something really special together. What happened?'

Her mate said, 'You spent it all!'

*

It was dusk in Gateshead's Saltwell Park and two young lovers were disturbed by the park keeper. She managed to escape but he had no option than to dive naked into an empty flower bed, and dragged soil over his naked body. He managed to cover all of his flesh except his cheeky bit which was sticking out of the ground.

Two pensioners well into their eighties spotted it, and old Cissie says, 'Do you know Bella,
  when I was 16 I was afraid of them
  when I was 20 I was putting up with them,
  when I was 30 I was enjoying them
  when I was 40 I was asking for them,
  when I was 50 I was paying for it,
  when I was 60 I was praying for it,
  when I was 70 I had forgotten about it,
and now here we are in our eighties and the bloody things are growing wild!'

*

Elsie and Gladys were chatting. 'I have a heck of a job waking up our George in the mornings,' said Elsie.

Gladdie said, 'Try rattling his trouser pockets!'

*

Hosting a party, Big John was trying to keep all his guests happy. He asked a teetotaller, 'Can I get you a bitter lemon?'

The reply he got was, 'No, I'd like a lot of lemon actually!'

*

My mate Denny told his wife that her tights were wrinkled. The problem was she wasn't wearing any!

*

My mate Denny's wife tells me that he is a lousy lover. How can she tell in a couple of minutes.

*

John from Whitley Bay spotted a young girl wearing fishnet stockings, bright red patent-leather shoes, a tiny sparkly boob tube and a tiny mini skirt. He walked up to her and said, 'I say, young lady, what would your mother say if she saw you here like this?'

The girl replied, 'She'd kill me, I'm on her corner!'

*

Why is it when a wife tells her husband there are 3,000,000,000 stars in the universe he'll believe her, but you tell him that a park bench has wet paint on it, he's got to touch it?

*

The footsteps that a son usually follows tend to be the ones his father thought that he'd covered up.

*

You can tell a woman's getting on when she's more concerned with how her shoes fit than her sweater!

*

A young lad spots an old nun having difficulty getting across the street. So he runs over and grabs her hand and guides her carefully through the masses of cars pouring down Newcastle Road in Sunderland.

The nun is very grateful and says, 'Thank you son, but what made you help me across the street?'

The young lad says, 'Any friend of Batman's is a friend of mine!'

*

Little Tony runs into his local Spar with a toilet roll and puts it on the counter saying, 'My mam says can she have our money back, because my Auntie Maureen didn't turn up!'

*

The rear seats of the bus to Blyth were nose to tail with children, fifteen of them, all screaming and shouting. As the lady paid their fares they ran amok. The driver said, 'Are they all yours or is this a picnic?'

The woman said, 'They're all mine and believe me it's no picnic!'

*

Eleven-year-old Brian was sitting on the train facing a pensioner. He was bored stiff, so he spent the entire thirty-minute journey between Newcastle and Sunderland chewing on some Wrigleys.

Just before they reached the station, the elderly lady says, 'It really was kind of you to talk to me right through the journey, but I'm afraid I'm rather deaf!'

*

Three brothers, Tom, Dick and Harry, all have big feet. Tom and Harry wear size fourteens and Dick wears size sixteens. They all went to a disco and while Dick was at the bar getting the drinks in, Tom and Harry got a couple of girls up to dance. They couldn't help but trample all over these poor girls' feet, their feet were just so large.

The girls both said, 'You both really do have enormous feet, don't you?'

Tom and Harry replied, 'If you think our feet are big, you should see the size of our Dick's!'

*

When a man steals your wife there is no better revenge than to let him keep her!

*

In ye olden Northern days Yorkshire had various huge mills, often run by cruel dictators more concerned with profit than with the staff. Such was the case in Welche's Woollen Mill in the North Riding. The male and female workers were housed in separate buildings so no hanky-panky could take place. The only opportunity they had to meet was either during their twenty-minute lunch break or at 8 p.m. after a twelve-hour shift.

Despite the problems Eric met Samantha and they fell in love.

So off went Eric to ask the mill owner for a few hours off work to get married. The owner was feeling benevolent and said, 'Alreet thou knows, but I expect thee back at work first thing Wednesday morning, and that goes for your lass too!'

So all of Monday in the women's mill Samantha was being kidded by the other girls, saying, 'Hey, you're going to get "what's what" tomorrow. Your drawers will be up and down like a Union Jack!' Everywhere Samantha went people said, 'She's going to get "what's what" tomorrow!'

However Samantha was a naive girl and didn't quite understand. Poor Eric was also being teased about his forthcoming wedding and he was as green as grass too. The lads shouted, 'Hey Eric you're going to get "what's what" tomorrow, your shirt will be up and down your back like a roller blind.'

Others cried, 'You looking forward to "what's what" tomorrow?'

Eric just blushed – he hadn't a clue what they meant!

So the day arrived, and wearing clothes handed down from his father, Eric was wed. Samantha looked wonderful in a white cotton dress sewn together by her nana, and they had saved for almost a year to afford a back room in a local pub for the night that would be their honeymoon.

They both put on their nightclothes and sat up in bed when Samantha said, 'Come on then, give me "what's what"!'

Eric shook his head and said, 'Hang on, you've got to give me "what's what"!'

'You're wrong,' said Samantha, 'the girls said *you* would give me "what's what"!'

'Impossible,' said Eric. 'The blokes said *you* would give *me* "what's what"!'

'I know,' said Samantha, 'it's one of those wedding-night pranks. They've hidden the "what's what" in the room. Have a look for it, Eric!'

So Eric looked around the room, and came up empty. He slumped dejectedly back on to the bed.

Then Samantha said, 'You haven't looked under my side of the bed. Lean over here and take a look!'

So obligingly Eric leaned across his new bride and at that moment his pyjama cord came undone and she saw his cheeky bits.

'What is that?' she asked.

'What's what?' said Eric.

Samantha grinned and said, 'You see, you had it all the time!'

*

A Bigg Market lad in his white shirt, stay-pressed trousers and hair gel visited his girlfriend's father to ask for her hand in marriage. The father knew he was a Bigg Market lad, so he didn't want his daughter involved. But she seemed keen, so the dad warned the boy of potential problems.

'I must tell you,' said the father, 'my daughter has acute angina.'

The Bigg Market lad says, 'Aye I know, and a great pair of gazonkas!'

*

A lady from Durham brought home triplets from Dryburn Hospital, and was met by her son at the door to the house. The five-year-old looked closely at the three babies, then turned to his dad and said: 'We better start ringing people now, these are going to be harder to get rid of than the kittens!'

*

Do you know why marriage is a fortress? Those in it want to get out, and those who are out want to get in!

*

Harry the accountant came in and shouted, 'Darling I'm home!' There was no answer. Harry thought that was a bit strange, and wondered where his wife could be. Suddenly he heard a panting noise coming from an upstairs bedroom. The husband rushed upstairs to find his wife lying on the bed with no clothes on, holding her left breast.

Harry shouted, 'What's going on, pet?'

The wife said, 'Darling, you've come home early and I'm having a heart attack!'

The husband ran downstairs screaming, 'Oh my

goodness, my darling wife,' and dialled 999. He was just about to ask for the ambulance when his young son came in and said, 'Dad, Uncle Peter is hiding in the wardrobe with nothing on.'

'What!' said Harry and rushed upstairs, tore into the bedroom, grabbed the wardrobe doors and flung them open. There stood Uncle Peter in the buff. Harry said, 'You dirty pig. My wife's having a heart attack and you're running around the house naked frightening the bairns!'

*

Why did the washing machine laugh?

It was taking the pee out of your knickers!

*

I asked my friend what the secret of his long-lasting marriage was. He said, 'We both go for a romantic meal every week. I have Italian, I don't know what she has!'

*

During a passionate clinch in his girlfriend's front room, Dave realised he needed to visit the netty. 'Excuse me Valerie, but I must pop to the smallest room in the house!'

'Oh you can't,' said Valerie. 'I'm not supposed to have my boyfriends in the house, and the toilet is next to my mam and dad's bedroom and they'll hear you!'

Dave looked very uncomfortable so Valerie said, 'Look just nip into the kitchen and use the sink. No one will be any the wiser!'

So Dave slid into the kitchen while Valerie put some make-up on. A couple of minutes later Dave stuck his head around the door and says, 'Have you got any paper?'

*

Long before the film *Fatal Attraction*, my mate Denny's wife always insisted that he ravish her up against the kitchen sink. It was the only way she could time her boiled egg to perfection.

*

In Darras Hall yuppies only get married if they are incompatible. That's if he has the income and she's pat-able!

*

The psychiatrist said to the old man, 'I am most dreadfully sorry, but your wife's mind has gone.'

The old fellow grinned, saying, 'I'm not surprised. She's been giving me a piece of it for long enough!'

*

My mate Denny said to his wife, 'Will you love me when I'm fat and bald?'

She said, 'Of course I do!'

*

My mate Denny was putting up an embroidered sign that he'd bought at a car boot sale. It read: 'BLESS OUR HAPPY HOUSE'.

His wife yelled, 'Don't put it on that wall, you stupid dope!'

*

Ray had a place near Gray's Monument in Newcastle. One day he was visiting his grandmother's grave in Jesmond when he put a huge bunch of roses in the graveside pot. He glanced to his left and spotted a small Japanese fellow with a primus stove, cooking some rice. Once it was cooked he placed it on a grave with a pair of chopsticks.

Ray smiled to himself, saying, 'When's your wife going to come up and eat that rice?'

The Japanese gent turned and said, 'When your granny comes up to smell those flowers!'

*

My mate Denny refuses to go to bed until a row is resolved. He's been awake since 1958.

TIM HEALEY

Tim is the man most people believe to be the North's best actor, having helped create one of the funniest TV shows of all time, *Auf Wiedersehen Pet* with Jimmy Nail and Kevin Whately. His TV successes continue with *The Boys from the Bush*. He's a very versatile performer with a great singing voice and a tremendous sense of humour, as brilliant on the live stage as he is on screen.

Recently I worked with him on the Telethon and he agreed to let an eight-stone German Shepherd chase and apprehend him. A terrific character.

Charlie was sitting at home watching the telly when there was a knock on the door, and on answering it he found it was the brush salesman.

'Hello sir, is the lady of the house in?'

'No,' said Charlie, 'she's at the shops. What d'ye want?'

'Well,' said the salesman, 'I have a special trial offer on brushes. I'd like to leave three samples, and I'll call back in a week and see if you'd like to buy them!'

'Sounds alreet to me,' said Charlie. He took the brushes and went back to his TV and his bottle of Pils.

The following week the salesman returned to the house, and said, 'Hello sir, is the lady of the house in?'

'No,' said Charlie. 'I told you last week she gans to the shops on a Monday.'

'I see,' said the salesman. 'Well, what did she think of the brushes?'

'She was quite impressed,' replied Charlie. 'The sweeping brush is very handy for cleaning up the scullery. She definitely wants the clothes brush because it gets the dog hairs off her dresses. But she really didn't like the toilet brush. She's tried to use it, but she still prefers toilet paper!'

*

My mate was going to buy his wife a waterbed but he was frightened they might drift apart.

*

Was it true your mate Denny bought mirrors for the ceiling above his bed? I think his wife wants to see the back of him!

PETER HETHERINGTON

Peter is a broadcaster who has worked for Great North Radio and other radio stations across the Yorkshire radio network, and is known throughout the North as 'Mr Smooth', playing his golden oldies. Peter has compiled a variety of musical collections on album, CD and cassette, often getting them into the national album charts. He is genuinely one of the nicest and most professional presenters I have ever had the good fortune to work with. Here is his favourite story:

Charlie buys a parrot and brings it home, and the next three months he spends all of his time saying 'Hello Polly', 'Polly wants a cracker', 'Hello' and various other phrases in a desperate attempt to get it to talk. Week after week the man refuses to give up, and decided that maybe the bird is bored, so each morning he takes the parrot out on his shoulder around the shops. Every person they pass says a few words to the parrot, hoping for some sign of it speaking, but all to no avail. Finally he's had enough. He grabs the parrot, sticks it in the pocket of his kagoule, and starts marching back to the pet shop.

He's crossing the road in the High Street when a car zooms down the road and the parrot yells, 'Watch Out!'

Too filled with anger, Charlie remains rooted to the spot and the car flattens him.

The parrot lands on the side of the road and says, 'Isn't that just ruddy typical? He spends months trying to teach me to talk, I finally say something and he doesn't listen!'

THE BAIRN SPEAKS OOT

Have you ever wondered what life would be like if you were a baby, yet you could communicate what you're feeling? Picture a little squidger sitting in his play pen, wearing his light blue Mickey Mouse nappy.

My mother refused to change me every five minutes when I was a bairn; she'd wait until I was too heavy to pick up, then get my Dad's wheelbarrow and take me out into the garden to help the compost heap!

Anyway over to little Alan.

Aren't mams and dads silly? They sit looking at us babies as if we're stupid. Sticking their sweaty fingers under our chins, going koochie-koochie-koo, who's Daddy's little angel, he's got his mother's eyes, his uncle's nose, his granny's scar etc. What a bunch of morons. We babies never get a decent conversation out of them. It's no wonder we try to wee-wee on them every time they pick us up.

Here I am with my light blue and pink bobble hat on, a light blue romper suit with Mickey Mouse kissing Minnie Mouse on my chest. I've little pink booties and a bib with Ed the Duck on it. Do you know why I am dressed like this? Because those rotten sods wouldn't give me any say whatsoever.

This is not to say I wasn't wanted as a baby. When I was born me dad handed all the cigars around. Mine was a bit strong but I finished it. When I was born everyone said I was very small – well, that's not surprising, for me mam and dad had only been married three weeks.

Do you know what gets right up my little snotty nose? It's people staring at me. I mean a lad never looks his best when he's wearing Pampers, now does he? They don't give you a chance to comb my hair or brush my toof! Then you're passed around like a ruddy parcel, and it's not always possible to summon up enough water to christen them all. If I can't manage it, I'm sick on a few as well. The only way it's safe to pick up this little Geordie is in an oilskin, sou'wester and a decent pair of wellies. Even though my dad is usually prepared I did manage to poo in his pocket on the day he went fishing!

Now what do you look forward to at dinnertime? A nice juicy steak, scampi and chips, a curry or a McDonald's? Sounds great, but my mam forces me to have my dinner off her chesties. I mean the milk's alright, but I've got to follow a bloke that smokes St Bruno!

When I can persuade them to give me something else, it's ham and apple purée, or cheese and coconut. They expect me to eat that. Eat it? I wouldn't sit in it! So it's back to the bristols with my head stuffed in her shirt. This is a problem because you miss what's happening in *Neighbours*. On the very few occasions that my dad dares to pick me up I occasionally catch a glimpse of his nipple. I was peckish once and gave it a try, but he was empty. It must be the recession, it's hitting everyone!

The least cough, or a poo that's a funny colour, and Dr Ram comes around – 'Docky Wocky' as my daft dad calls him. Why is it that all my mates' dads feed them by waving a spoonful of slop at them and then saying, 'Open up your tunnel there's a choo choo coming!'? I mean where is he going to stick that spoon? Is it any wonder we always fill our nappy at the very thought?

Parents are a real pain. They make you go to sleep when you're not tired, then they wake you up when you're fast asleep. Is it any wonder that I spend half the night screaming my head off after such emotional cruelty? I am only likkle you know! Then one of these bleary-eyed, smelly-breathed big'uns comes in and sings a lullaby. 'Rock-A-Bye Baby' is my favourite, it's a very simple tune. I think it's one of Paul McCartney's.

So I'm never tired when they put me to bed, and I can't sleep. How can anybody get rest when your mam and dad are grunting and panting? I mean, why do they leave it that late before moving around the bedroom furniture? They get so excited about it too! I hear my mam yelling 'Yes yes yes' . . . I mean, come on mother, what difference does it make where my dad puts your wardrobe? Once I crawled into their room and my dad must have been dreaming that he was on a bouncy castle, 'cos he was leaping up and down on my mam. When I asked him what he thought he was doing he said 'I'm playing circuses.' Now what the hell did he mean by that?

72

I do have a bit of a personal problem. It's very embarrassing. When I go to sleep, sometimes my kidneys don't. I nearly drowned my teddy Giles! Once I was in bed with my daddy and he woke up to find out that I'd widdled in his ear. My mam said it was a dweadful accident, my nana said I just couldn't help myself. Personally, though, I thought it was a hell of a shot!

Something else I'm unhappy with – why do mams and dads always applaud when I poo in my potty? Then my dad grabs it while it's still hot and shows everybody in the house, and then they all clap too. Adults are weird. If I burp dead loud everybody says well done, yet if my Uncle Bill does it they call him a pig!

Last week my dad bought a book called *Child Psychology* – he hits me with it!

I was an accident, you know. My dad says he was just talking to my mam and something came up in the conversation. Not long after I was born my mam and dad fought lots. My dad wanted to play a game called 'Mucky Filth'. I don't know where he keeps it, it's not in the cupboard next to the Scrabble and Monopoly. My mam said no, she didn't want to play. My dad was really desperate, then he started to look at my Auntie Betty with a wicked glint in his eyes! I think my mammy must have lent the game to her!

My mammy told me when she had me in her tummy that she had funny cravings, like eating coal, putting mixed pickles in with her ice cream, or eating jellied eels with semolina. It doesn't surprise me that she was sick every morning.

Last night my daddy took me in the bath for the

first time. He put ducks on the surface and I noticed that he's deformed. He's got two big spots underneath his widdler. I didn't want to say anything, but I'm sure he must have noticed. I've seen some spots in my time, but if ever two needed squeezing it was them!

All things considered it's not bad being a baby. At least you get lots of cuddles!

STEVE COLMAN

Considered by many, including myself, to be Britain's top breakfast show presenter and star of the national BBC television series *Knock Knock*, Steve is as over the top as they come. He came up with a story of the Old West.

Two cowboys, Buck and Hal, were riding along the plains of Arizona when suddenly in the horse's rearview mirror Hal spotted a Red Indian riding towards them.

Buck says, 'Tell me how close he is.'

Hal says, 'He's about one foot tall to look at.'

'Hell's bells,' says Buck, 'that is close. Let's get out of here!' And they slapped their horses and galloped away.

About a mile later Buck yells, 'Hal, where's that Injun now?'

Hal looks and shouts, 'He's getting closer he looks about two foot tall now!'

So they tore away even faster.

Yet another mile down the road Hal shouts, 'He's getting closer, he's about three feet tall now. No, it's four feet . . . now it's five feet!' So they whipped their horses into a frenzy and rode into Yoohoo Gulch, pulling up outside the sheriff's office.

They told the sheriff and then popped into the saloon for a drink to calm them down. As they stood at the bar knocking back four fingers of red-eye, the saloon doors swung open and in walked the biggest Red Indian you've ever seen. He must have been close to seven feet tall.

'Shoot him, Hal!' says Buck.

'No, I can't do it!' says his friend.

'For heaven's sake, shoot!' screamed Buck.

Hal replied, 'I can't do it, I've known him since he was so high!'

PAUL FROST

The star of Tyne Tees Television and host of *Northern Life*, along with the bubbly Pam Royle. He has long been one of television's best anchor-men, with a flair for both the serious and the witty.

During the Telethon he worked non-stop through the entire weekend, and never made a slip, a testament to his skill and professionalism. Not to be outdone, Paul came up with a joke he invented himself:

What do you call a Scottish pop group who are hard of hearing?

What? What? What?

NORMAN WISDOM

I was thrilled to bits on hearing that Tyne Tees Television had managed to get the great Norman Wisdom to appear on my chat show *Robson's People*. It didn't bother me at all that he's a canny age, as he is a star of immense proportions, one of the few that makes you laugh without saying a word. None of the production team could wait to meet him, and when security buzzed us to say he'd arrived, there was an excited air of anticipation. One of my researchers, Ann-Marie Burnham, went down to reception, and witnessed this tiny man who appeared to be totally 'out of it'. He could barely talk, and came across as very frail. He could barely walk, and Ann-Marie gingerly led him towards the lift, and it took almost ten minutes to cover less than fifteen feet.

Ann-Marie got in the lift and held the button and waited for Norman to shuffle aboard. He never appeared, so Ann-Marie stuck her head out of the lift to find Norman bounding up the stairs, taking them two at a time.

He's a great prankster and he's got all his buttons on. To entertainment purists like myself, being involved in comedy on screen with Norman is as good as working with Chaplin or Laurel and Hardy. He really is *that* good! God bless him.

TONY HODGE

For years Tony Hodge was the drummer with a manic Northern rock band called the Piranha Brothers, and we became very pally. His bald head butting the symbols and his smiling face was the highlight of many a show. His other great love was acting, and through his links with Equity he had auditioned and obtained dozens of 'bit' parts. Once I had a hilarious evening looking at all of his bits on a video cassette.

'You see that soldier there, right at the back . . . the one wearing the gasmask . . . in the tunnel . . . lying face down . . . that's me, you know!' he would say.

Occasionally you'd catch a glimpse of him, but blink and you'd miss it.

He'd been in the entertainment business for over twenty years and you begin to think that with luck like that when your ship eventually does come in, you'll be at the airport!

However, my great belief is that if you work hard enough you'll get where you deserve to be. I was thrilled to bits on hearing that Tony had won a small part on the national children's television soap *Byker Grove*. Very soon Tony had proven himself to be a 'regular' and now people recognise him in the street and I sincerely hope he can go on to even better things. He's one of the nicest lads I've ever met.

Being bald isn't too bad, he once told me: 'I can comb my hair with a wet shammy!'

Ask Tony for a joke and you get a batch . . . here they are:

One lovely sunny day an old man was driving his Lada down a long dual carriageway. There was very little traffic and the man was really enjoying himself. The happiness was swift to subside when the Lada's engine began to cough and splutter, eventually coming to an abrupt halt. The man got out and looked under his bonnet only to have his worst fears realised. The rubber band had snapped! It was knackered!

He was about to despair when a red Ferrari pulled up beside him and the driver swung out and walked towards him. In an accent that would even sound posh in Whickham, he asked the Lada driver if he would like a tow to the nearest garage.

The Lada driver accepted gratefully, and proceeded to tie the two vehicles together.

The two cars proceeded to drive at a sedate 30 m.p.h. along the road, and the Lada driver was steering and enjoying his trip out in the summer sun. It was the first time since buying his Lada that he'd been able to hear the car radio! Unfortunately the peace was soon shattered when a white Mazda sports car pulled up level with the Ferrari. The Mazda driver didn't see the tow rope between the cars and blew a raspberry at the Ferrari driver and yelled, 'I bet my twin turbo can blow you away!'

The Ferrari driver couldn't resist it, and when the Mazda driver slammed his foot down on the accelerator and zoomed up the road in a cloud of dust it was more than the Ferrari driver could take. He whopped the car into third gear and took off, accelerating to catch up. He reached 130 m.p.h. and still he hadn't caught the Mazda.

Meanwhile the poor Lada driver was bouncing about on the end of the rope flashing his lights to alert the Ferrari driver, whose mind was now only on the Mazda in front. He was totally oblivious to the problems he was causing the Lada behind.

The three cars roared past Seghill Service Station and Steve the gaffer turned to his dad and said, 'Now there's something you don't see every day. There's a Mazda RX7 doing at least 150 m.p.h. with a red Ferrari trying to catch him!'

'That's nowt,' said his dad.

'But that's not all, Dad,' said Steve. 'There's a little Lada on *their* tail, flashing his lights so they can let him past!'

*

Tony once saw an advert in his local paper that read: 'I have lost my puppy dog. One ear, one eye, three legs, broken tail. Answers to the name Lucky!'

*

Tony also tells of three squaddies in the Gulf during the hostilities and they're all sweltering under the hot sun. They decided that they would play a game, selecting one item each that they would choose if they could pick anything.

'It's so hot I'd love a pint of ice-cold Guinness!' said the first.

'Me,' said the second, 'I'm so dry I'd have a litre of ice-cold lager!'

The third surprised them all by saying, 'Well, I would quite fancy a car door!'

The other lads couldn't understand so their mate added, 'Then I could wind the window down and get a lovely cold breeze!'

*

Tony's final joke was about his younger days when his head was used as a model for the German helmets.

In 1916 the First World War was well on its murderous way. The German army had many victories and its trenches were well into France. At this time however an eerie silence fell on the two opposing armies. On one side were the British Tommies, and in the other trenches the German Hun. Not one shot had been fired for a week and the British colonel saw the fighting edge of his troops melting away. He knew that something had to be done. He called his best rifle shot and told him to find a spot where he could see the trenches of the Germans clearly. He was then to call out the most common German name and when he was answered he was to shoot them!

So out he crawled into No-Man's-Land and took up his position and shouted 'Hans!'

Up pops a German soldier who shouts '*Ja*!'

BANG!

The sniper crawled back to his lines and reported to his commanding officer that his mission was a success, so out he goes again the following day. He finds another spot and shouts 'Hans!'

Another head sticks up and says '*Ja*.'

BANG!

Every day for almost a month the same thing happened, and every time it worked. Morale had never been higher when the German High Command felt that they must try and lift their soldiers.

'These British are very clever,' said General Von Eifler, 'but ve can play zis game too. Tonight ven it is dark our sniper must crawl out to where we can see their lines and shout the most common of English names, Tommy, and zen shoot him!'

So that night the German sniper took his position,

waited until he was set, and shouted 'Tommy!' There was no reply.

He yelled again, 'Tommy!' Still no one responded.

Then he stood up and shouted as loud as he could, '*Tommy*!!'

A voice came back, 'Is that you, Hans?'

The German said '*Ja.*'

BANG!

HOWAY THE LADS AND LASSES

The North East is a hotbed of seething sporting loyalties. When Sunderland were beaten in the FA Cup final real Northern supporters cheered them for a great performance, yet there were die-hard Newcastle fans who supported Liverpool that day.

With Gateshead International Stadium, the great Northern football teams Middlesbrough, Sunderland, Berwick, Hartlepool, Darlington, Leeds, Newcastle, Blyth Spartans, Carlisle, and many others, we have such a great heritage. So here's a vast array of dodgy sporting jokes, from all camps!

Bald swimming star Duncan Goodhew was visiting a Northern pool to teach youngsters when he dived in. As soon as he hit the water his swimming trunks came off and he floated to the surface bum first. Everybody thought he'd split his head open!

*

Did you hear about the frisky stockbroker who went golfing with faulty condoms? He got a hole in one, lost a ball, and got a birdie in the club.

*

What does Newcastle United have in common with Count Dracula?

They're both afraid of crosses.

*

What is the difference between Hartlepool United and a teabag?

A teabag stays in the cup longer.

*

A tip for all teams. The best way to win a football match is to equalise before your opponents score!

*

Two pals were at Ayresome Park, Middlesbrough and one lad said, 'Hey, I'm bursting to gan to the netty, but this place is so full, I'll never find my way back if I go to the toilet block.'

So his mate said, 'Now, look at that bloke in front of you, he's got wellies on. Just do it in them!'

The pal was shocked, saying, 'Give over, he's bound to feel it!'

His friend said, 'Well you didn't, did you?'

*

What do you call an upside-down Reliant Robin with a football inside?

A whistle!

*

What's the difference between Darlington's goalkeeper and a turnstile?

A turnstile only lets them in one at a time!

*

If you have a referee in football and an umpire in tennis, what do you have in bowls?

Soup!

*

Why did the bank manager become a goalkeeper?

He was a good saver!

*

I have a lot in common with boxers – I'm never up before ten.

*

There is a sign on the wall in one of Newcastle's swimming pools that reads 'No Petting'. I wonder why you never see a sign in any of the nightclubs that reads 'No Swimming'?

*

One of Billy Hardy's Sunderland stablemates was boxing against a huge American at the Crowtree Leisure Centre and for the first three rounds he was getting well chinned. His eyes were puffy and bruised, his lip was cut, his ear looked like a cauliflower and his manager said, 'Don't worry son, he hasn't touched you, he hasn't laid a glove on you!'

After two more rounds this poor lad was pounded into stewing steak. He crashed down on to the stool, totally exhausted and panting like a spaniel in heat, only to hear his manager say, 'Don't worry son, he hasn't touched you, he hasn't laid a glove on you.'

The boxer said, 'Listen boss, do me a favour. Keep an eye on the ring, because there's someone out there beating the shit out of me!'

*

At one of the really big engineering factories on the Team Valley Trading Estate in Gateshead, they play dominoes every lunchtime. There was this lad Billy Richardson who always won every single game, and all the other lads were getting well sick of him. One day he was boasting and bragging about how great a domino player he was when they turned on him. Without ceremony they tipped him upside down and proceeded to ram all the dominoes up his backside. He was in agony and ran out of the factory, racing all the way to the nearest doctor in Dunston, kicked open the front door, burst through a full surgery and crashed into the doctor's room.

The doctor turned around and said, 'Don't you ever knock?'

*

I was actually going to be a boxer, I had a terrific rabbit punch. The problem was the RSPCA wouldn't let me fight rabbits.

*

I was sitting in the Bank Top Toby Grill restaurant near Kenton when I struck up a conversation with a man in his late thirties. As things turned out he was a boxer, and he wanted to have another crack at the championship. He kept telling me, 'Alan, I can beat Rocky McIllhatton, I can beat him, I know I can. McIllhatton is a big bloke, but I know I can beat him. If I had the chance I'd paste that Rocky McIllhatton all over the ring!'

I said, 'There's only one problem.'

He asked what that was.

I replied, 'You are Rocky McIllhatton!'

*

What's red and white and slides down the table?
Sunderland FC.

*

Why is the grass at White Hart Lane so lush and green?

Because they put six million pounds' worth of crap on it every week!

*

One boxer from Birtley was having trouble sleeping, so I persuaded him to try counting sheep. The only

86

problem was as soon as he got to nine he would jump up.

*

I attended one of Glenn McCrory's fights and during a match before the main event a little lad from Stanley was getting a pasting from some fighter from London. A voice shouts out from the back of the hall: 'Dougie, knock him out and you might get a draw!'

*

A school from Leeds took a party of schoolchildren to York races, and after they'd spent their time enjoying the atmosphere the lady teacher took the little infant boys to the toilet before getting on the bus for the trip home. One by one she unzipped each boy's trousers, helped him hold his party sausage, then sent him on to the bus. She'd just finished helping the last one when she said, 'All right, get on the bus, we're going home now.'

The lad said, 'I'd love to pet, but I'm a jockey in the 3.30.'

*

A leading tennis player walks into a pub after losing the Wimbledon final and spots a good-looking blonde having a drink. After a swift drink they end up back in his hotel room, and ultimately in bed. As she was undressing him she noticed he had 'View From' written down his arm. The blonde asked why he'd had that done. The tennis player replied, 'I get £25,000 in sponsorship from them.'

He then took his trousers off and she saw the word 'Puma' written down each leg. Once again the blonde enquired as to what that was all about. 'I

87

get £15,000 for each leg from my sponsors,' answered the tennis star.

When he removed his underpants she spotted the words AIDS tattooed on his manhood. 'I'm not touching that,' she said.

The tennis star said, 'Don't worry – if you play your cards right that'll say Adidas!'

*

I don't gamble on anything after a visit to Gosforth Park one day with my dad, when he lost our rent money. He said to my mam, 'That horse would have run that race, if it hadn't kept looking back for his plough!'

*

What flies out of your wardrobe at 125 m.p.h.?
Stirling Moth.

*

A local stable-owner in Cumbria was so sick of a horse called Flashpoint losing its races that he decided to give the horse one final warning. He said, 'Listen you useless Galawa (horse), if you div not win today's race, I guarantee you that tomorrow morning at four o'clock you'll be delivering the milk, and you'll be doing that for the rest of your career!'

The race started. Everybody began at a fair old lick, then Flashpoint started slowing down to barely a trot. The jockey was standing up in the saddle clagging him with his whip.

The horse finally stopped and said, 'Pack that in, will you? Do you not realise I've got to be up at four o'clock tomorrow morning?'

*

My mate Denny once bet on a horse in the Grand

National that was so slow the jockey's wife sued him for desertion.

*

What sits in your dressing table, yet is capable of 160 m.p.h.?

Hondapants.

*

During the Milk Race, Newcastle city centre is at an absolute standstill, as the world's leading cyclists tear around one of the finest courses anywhere in the world.

A poser from Darras Hall was out for a spin in his Ferrari when he saw one of these cyclists and decided to swank past him doing 60 m.p.h. He chuckled to himself as he did so, but was surprised when suddenly there was a tapping on his side window. He looked around to see the cyclist peddling like fury. On winding down the window the cyclist said, 'Sorry to bother you, but have you got a light? I'm dying for a ciggy.'

The Ferrari driver put his foot down and accelerated to 90 m.p.h., thinking 'That'll sort him.'

Yet within a minute there was a tapping at his side window and the cyclist, legs all a-blur, shouted, 'Howay kidder, I only want a ruddy light!'

The Ferrari driver was well sick, and slammed his foot down onto the floor and roared up the Great North Road at 148 m.p.h. He looked in his mirror and there behind him was the cyclist, and he was gaining all the time. As they whizzed past Morpeth the biker was by his side, matching the car mile for mile. Once again he tapped on the car window, yelling, 'Look, can you give me a light for my cigarette or not?'

The Ferrari driver said, 'You maniac, you'll kill yourself.'

The cyclist replied, 'Hadaway, I only smoke about four a day, man!'

*

Never marry a tennis player, love means nothing to them!

*

My dad always took me fishing to Ford Castle in Northumberland and on the way home I asked him if fish grow fast. My mam said, 'I should say so – every time your dad describes one it grows another foot!'

*

Never marry a golf player, they prefer to play around.

*

Never marry a footballer, they always want to get the first leg over.

*

I played in a celebrity rugby match against a homosexual team to raise money for charity. They had four tries and a conversion.

*

Is it really true the Newcastle fencing team got knocked out of the national championships because they ran out of creosote?

*

My mate Denny loves sport and once I found him with a well-oiled bat. In fact he married her!

*

A lad from Annfield Plain was poaching near Kielder. He'd caught a duck, and was sitting at the edge of the water plucking it, when the bailiff came walking by. The lad hurled the duck into the water and sat there looking guilty with feathers all over him.

'And what do you think you're doing?' asked the bailiff.

The lad brushed more feathers off his lap and said, 'I've just brought my pet duck up here for a swim and I'm holding his clothes!'

*

Now golfers are a strange breed, and nothing is more important to them than the game. One day a golfer sliced one of his drives so badly that it flew out of the fairway and crashed into the crowd, killing a man instantly.

The golfer said, 'This is awful, what on earth can I do?'

His partner said, 'Well, I think you should keep your head lower, and try to keep your elbow a little stiffer!'

*

Before one of my TV shows, Frank Carson guested at Sunderland cricket club and was in fits of laughter watching two crows playing football with a golf ball. He actually phoned Tyne Tees, but reporter Duncan Wood didn't believe it was Frank Carson, and thought that someone was drunk. Apparently it has been known for crows to steal golf balls during a game.

*

Mark Forrest is a really fit lad. He runs five miles a day, doesn't eat sweets, red meat or dairy products, sleeps eight hours a night, has cycled across Europe, doesn't drink or smoke, never drinks coffee or fizzy

91

drinks, works out and doesn't mess with the wrong sort of women.

We were discussing his lifestyle and my mate Denny says, 'One day he's going to feel really stupid!'

I asked what he meant and Denny replied, 'How's he going to explain lying in a bed dying of nothing!'

*

Actually my mate Denny could've been a Formula One racing champion if he hadn't kept pulling into the pits to ask directions!

*

Lady shot-putters try really hard to look attractive, but for some of them it isn't easy. So one day this girl was so desperate for a man she took her dog out for a walk and decided to go for broke.

She walked into the Bridge Hotel, which was packed with men having a drink, and shouted, 'If any of you can guess the age of my dog, I'll take you home and make mad passionate love to you!'

One wag at the bar shouts, 'Is he 236?'

The shot-putter says, 'That's close enough for me!'

PAUL GASCOIGNE

Paul Gascoigne is a genuine lad from Dunston that the media pester to death in search of any scandal. I'd met Paul on a number of occasions including a visit to a housing estate in Newcastle when a loving family were forced to bring Christmas early for a brave, terminally ill little boy. Paul was magnificent. No press, no publicity, just him doing what he thought was right.

Yet after his famous transfer to Italy was announced the tabloid harassment he suffered became ridiculous. Once I was hosting a live radio party on air, asking callers to ring in with a song or a joke, and to my surprise Paul Gascoigne was at the end of the line. It seems he was at his mam's enjoying a party and had been listening in and wanted to join in the fun. So we had a bit of a chat, he told everybody how much he was looking forward to Italian football. I told him he either had to sing or tell a joke, so he proceeded to sing his hit record 'Geordie Boys' without actually using proper notes. Later in the evening another lad from the party rang in and started telling a joke that was in bad taste – spurred on by someone in the back-ground!

Be honest, isn't that the kind of joke we all hear at everybody's party?

Well, I cut off the gag, as it was Christmas, never the time for a tasteless joke on air. But the following day the tabloids had hyped it into 'GAZZA IN RELIGIOUS JOKE FURY'.

The joke was never aired. The beginning of it was heard, but the punchline never went out. Still the press had gathered churchmen to have a go at Paul. Paul never told the joke! Nobody at home even heard the joke!

The night before, Paul had appeared live onstage with me during the panto *Sherlock Holmes and the Christmas Curse* and donated in front of a capacity crowd an entire performance to an old people's home and underprivileged children. The papers never even mentioned it. Doesn't that speak volumes about the standards of some journalists?

But no reason why that should get in the way of a good sensationalist story.

So on Paul's behalf I include his joke: 'The tabloid press!'

FRANK BRUNO

Over the years I've played in Frank Bruno's celebrity team at Gateshead International Stadium raising money for Metro FM's charity appeal. Watching Frank Bruno pounding down a football pitch with Linford Christie under one arm and John Regis under the other was one of my all-time sporting highlights!

My football career had a very shaky start. In a dressing room full of celebrities and professional players we were dishing out the positions we would play. Dennis Waterman shouted, 'I'll have the Number 9.'

'Damn,' said I under my breath. After all he was a guest in the North, so I'll pick up whatever number was left. I didn't mind as long as it wasn't in defence, or on the left-hand side, as I am firmly right-footed.

They handed me the left-back's shirt, and told me that our back line consisted of myself, Steve Coppell, the manager of Crystal Palace and ex-Manchester United and England star, and, in the middle, Bobby Moore, ex-West Ham and England captain who lifted the World Cup in 1966.

We were playing against Steve Cram's athletes with a front line that featured Daley Thompson, Linford Christie, John Regis and countless other star athletes, none of them exactly short of pace.

Did they run at Steve Coppell?

Did they run at Bobby Moore?

Or did they run at the idiot with ginger hair who stood as if he had both feet down one leg of his shorts?

I tried to catch them, but my tackles were so late they had scored and returned to their own half before I'd got up.

Were it not for Frank, we would never have held the game together. Players bounced off him, and they never tackled him in case he got annoyed. His presence is such that it's worth a couple of goals just to have him threaten the opposition.

In some games we were up against really skilful

players like our very own Paul Gascoigne. I managed to nick the ball off him early in the game, and from that point on he booted me all over the park. I ended up with more bruises on my backside than a one-legged can-can dancer!

At one game I pulled Frank to one side and interviewed him for the near capacity crowd asking, 'Why do you make the North your second home? You're up here for the Great North Run, the Great North Bike ride, the Great North Walk, Sport Aid and the Charity Appeal?'

He replied, 'Well, the weather is so hot, and I need to top up my tan!'

JACK CHARLTON

Jack Charlton from Ashington is one of the greatest footballing heroes to come out of the North East. Since he and his brother Bobby were taught to kick a ball by their mother, Jack has had 35 England caps, played on the 1966 World Cup team and managed Sheffield Wednesday. Now of course he manages the Republic of Ireland's football team, and he took the time to send me this great story from Dublin:

A friend of mine called Mac Murrey phoned me one day to say he was coming to Dublin on business, and as we had a game that evening he wanted to know could I get him a ticket. Of course, I said. After the game I got a car to take us to a building site on the far side of the city. When we arrived there Mac went to the Portacabin to ask for a Joe

Murphy. 'Over the side of the site,' he was told, 'just ask and they will get him for you.'

On our way over the site we came to two holes in the ground, full of water. Between the two holes was a pile of stones, and sat on the top was a little Irishman with a pumping machine. The pipe was in one hole, and the water coming out was running over the ground and into the other hole. 'It's going into the other hole,' shouted Mac, 'and it's probably filtering back into the first again.'

The little Irishman looked up. 'Mr Murrey,' he said, 'this is my hole. That one's got bugger all to do with me.'

That's why I love the Irish!

JAYNE McKENZIE

This lady is the raunchiest singer you have ever heard, the finest female vocalist in the North in my opinion. She has appeared on tour with dozens of huge stars, and performed in panto with me. She oozes sex appeal, and you could never take her home to meet your folks – you'd not be able to trust your father!

Who was the last boxer to pooh himself in the ring?
  'Geordie Lad', Crufts 1991.

LITTLE WASTERS, BAIRNS AND TEENY GALOOTS

When he was little my mate Denny was asked what kind of job he wanted. He told his teacher, 'I want to be a lollipop man, 'cos you don't have to start work until you're sixty.'

*

My dad was so mean that when he got married it was in our back garden so the chickens could eat the rice!

*

'Daddy,' said the little bairn, 'I want to get married!'

'Oh,' said his dad with a smile, 'and just who do you want to marry?'

'Granny,' said the lad.

'Hang aboot,' said his dad, 'you don't think that I'd let you marry my mother, do you?'

'Why not?' said his son. 'You married mine!'

*

I visited a primary school in Sunderland, and after I gave a bit of a talk to the bairns, I gathered them around and we swapped jokes. These children were aged between five and seven. One lad whose name was Geoffrey said, 'A dad was in the bath with his son and the boy pointed at his thingie and asked, "What's that, Daddy?" His father said, "Oh that's my hedgehog!" The boy looked for a while then said, "It's got a big willy for a hedgehog hasn't it!"'

And we think these little ones div not understand?

*

What's the difference between people from the North East and babies?

Babies have an excuse for not being able to talk properly.

*

A young father was trying to explain to his five-year-old son that his wife was expecting again. He said, 'Now pay attention, son, because one day soon a stork from Heaven is going to fly on to the roof of this house, come down the chimney and bring your mummy a present from God!'

The young lad says, 'I hope it doesn't give me mam a fright, 'cos she's pregnant, you know!'

*

A group of little girls were talking in the playground and one had just told them that she had a new little brother. They all asked how old he was, to which the girl answered: 'He is so new he hasn't got a number yet!'

*

What is the difference between snots and spinach?

You can't get children to eat spinach!

*

Little Barry, aged eight, walks into the living room with his girlfriend and shouts 'Hoy Dad, can Shirley and me have babies?'

The dad says 'Of course not.'

At this the young lad says, 'Champion, so it's back to your place and we'll give the chemist a miss then!'

*

Two little lads hung around until the end of the biology lesson to have a private word with the teacher. When the class had cleared, Ian asks, 'Sir, which one is that walks sideways? Is it crabs or lobsters?'

The teacher replied, 'It's crabs that walk sideways.'

Ian turned to his pal and said, 'See, I told you you've got lobsters!'

*

An anonymous letter from Hartlepool read: 'Dear Alan, a little girl was playing in the park with her dad when he noticed a man walking his dog. Her father said, "Look over there, there's a King Charles!"

The little lass said "Yes, Daddy, and he's walking his dog!"'

*

Some kids are right worky tickets! Once when I was at school I refused point-blank to do my essay. So the teacher kept me back and made me write out a story in not less than 50 words. I wrote, 'When I returned home last night I could not find my cat. So I went to my front door and shouted, "Pussy Pussy!"

To get his revenge the teacher made me stay in

100

the following night missing another paper round. This time he said, 'Robson, I want you to describe in detail every single thing that happened in your last school cricket match!'

After two minutes I handed him my finished paper. It read: 'Rain Stopped Play.'

*

One day a group of kids were hanging around outside the chip shop on Adelaide Terrace in Elswick and one said, 'My grandad is 98, you know.'

Another lad shouts, 'That's nowt, my granda is 102!'

Then a little girl whispers, 'So what? My granda is going strong at 203 . . . 203 Hugh Gardens.'

*

A little bairn and her 87-year-old nana were driving into Durham. There were cars everywhere, all full of dopy speeding drivers in XR2s, never indicating, flashing lights and squealing their brakes on those pratty handbrake turns.

The little lass says, 'Nana, don't drive around those corners so fast, I'm getting frikened!'

'Well, just do what I do,' said grandma, 'and shut your eyes!'

*

There was a mother-and-baby group at a Newcastle community centre and the local Kung Fu instructor walked into the main hall and spotted a pretty mother cradling a tiny baby. 'Bloody hell,' says the man, 'what an ugly little bugger he is!'

The mother burst into tears and after a few moments the caretaker of the hall saw her crying, and walked towards her.

'What's wrong, hinny?' he asked.

'It was a man, he came up and said something really insulting to me!' she said, sobbing into a wedge of Kleenex tissues.

'Hang on then, pet,' and off he went, returning five minutes later with a tray full of stuff. He put the tray down beside her and said, 'Now here's a cup of tea that'll put you right, and there's a banana for your monkey!'

*

Did you hear about the Mexican fireman who called his two sons José and Hose B?

*

A stunning-looking fifteen-year-old girl was taunting and teasing her boyfriend at the school gates one day, and asked him, 'Am I vain, do you think?'

Her lad, knowing he was on to a good thing, said, 'No, of couse not!'

She added, 'Because girls as beautiful as me usually are!'

*

A young mother took her ten-year-old son for his first visit to the Spiritualists. The medium spotted the child at once and brought him right to the front of the service. 'Little boy, who would you like us to contact for you?'

The little lad said 'My Granda Willis please!'

So the medium went into a trance. Her eyes glazed over, and then in a very deep voice she boomed across the darkened room: 'I am here, son, this is your Granda Willis. Now what do you want to ask me?'

The little lad replied, 'What are you doing in Heaven, Granda? You're not even dead yet!'

*

We know that posh people are tighter with their money than those of us with nowt. Is that why posh people's houses are all double-glazed, so their bairns can't hear the ice-cream vans?

*

While Danny's dad was at the football match his mother decided to have a run with the bairns to Edinburgh Zoo. They had a grand day climbing the hill, and the children were full of all the wonderful creatures that they had seen. 'Dad,' said four-year-old Danny, 'I saw the heffalump, and it had a tail at both ends!'

'Did it, son?' chipped in his father.

'Yes,' said Danny, 'and it was wagging them both from side to side.'

'Smashing,' replied his dad.

'But you'll never guess what happened next. It picked up a cream cake, and you'll never guess where he shoved it!'

*

What did the policeman say to his tummy?

'You're under a-vest!'

*

What did the policeman's son say when his mother asked who wanted some chips?

'Me Ma Me Ma Me Ma Me Ma!'

*

In a history lesson the teacher asked the class to name an American state with the letter P and H. One young lad shouts, 'Pearl Harbor.'

The teacher replied, 'No, Philadelphia.'

The lad said, 'Hadaway, that's a cheese spread!'

After the teacher explained that Philadelphia was a state before its name was taken for the cheese, then he added, 'Pearl Harbor has never been a state.'

The lad, not to be outdone, shouts, 'It was after the Japanese bombed it!'

*

A young lad from South Shields was walking down the road when he spotted a huge pile of doggy doo in the middle of the path.

'That looks like dog poo,' he said. He scooped up a lump and held it under his nose, and said, 'It certainly smells like dog poo!'

Then he takes a bite out of it and says, 'And it tastes like dog poo! I'm ruddy pleased I didn't step in it!'

*

A young lad was sitting on his father's knee and the old fellow said, 'Listen carefully, son, I'm going to tell you about the birds and the bees.'

The young lad says, 'Divvn't bother, Dad. Just tell me about lasses!'

*

One young lad goes up to his grandad and says, 'What's a weapon then?'

The old bloke says 'Well, it's something that you fight with.'

The bairn thought awhile and replied, 'You mean like Granma?'

*

One day a young lad was in his garden on the Ridges in North Shields and he had a hold of this big slippy slimy worm, and he tugged and tugged and tugged at it. His grandfather was walking along the road and spotted the lad yanking at this worm, finally dislodging it, and falling on his backside.

'Hey Johnny, it isn't very clever disturbing Mr Worm like that!' shouted the old man. 'If you can get it back into its hole I'll give you a pound coin!'

At this the young lad ran into the house. Two minutes later he returned with the worm as stiff as a pencil, and in a single action pushed it back into the ground.

'That's amazing,' puffed the old grandad. 'How did you do that?'

'Oh, it was nothing,' replied the grandson. 'I just got some of me mam's hair lacquer and sprayed it until it was hard, then put it back in the soil.'

So as good as his word, the old man paid the young lad and went home.

Two days later the grandad passed the garden again. The young lad was playing with his Nintendo, and the old man called him over.

'Here, son,' said the grandfather, 'here's a fiver.'

The boy said, 'But Grandad, you already paid me for the worm!'

The old man said, 'No, this is off your grandma!'

SIR JIMMY SAVILE OBE

What can you say about Sir James, every broadcaster's hero, who has done everything the rest of
the business aspires to? Doing this often in a world
where having Northern roots is prone to hold you
back, but Jimmy has smashed that antiquated
mould. His radio show 'Savile's Travels' is still head
and shoulders above the rest and drawing listeners
in their millions. His TV work includes *Jim'll Fix
It*, and as he's been a colleague of mine on Metro
FM, Jim was kind enough to fix it for me by giving
me his selection.

Jim says, 'Because my jokes are of a wide diversity
I think it's safer to send two children's jokes.'

I eat my peas with honey
I've done it all my life.
It makes them taste quite funny,
But it keeps them on my knife!

*

What is a slug?
  A snail without a mortgage.

*

'I did have a variety of other jokes,' says Jim, 'but these can only be sent out under a plain cover and are not for general public consumption. I usually wear a mask when I tell them!'

INNOCENCE IN TROUBLED TIMES

An eight-year-old boy had an essay to write about the recession, and after his tea he asked his folks how the economic climate had affected the home. His dad said, 'Well son, that television is from the catalogue and we haven't finished paying for it yet. The carpets and three-piece suite is on HP from Dickens, the house has a mortgage which means we still owe the building society £35,000 on it, we owe the paper shop £22, we can't afford our Poll Tax, the water bill's due, and the electric bill, so really we owe a fortune!'

So the bairn says, 'Thank you!'

At this his mam says, 'Look Philip, you stay down here and write your essay, your dad and me are going upstairs for a lie-down.'

Well, about an hour later the little lad crept up the stairs so as not to wake up his parents, and he heard his mam yell, 'Oh Jack, I'm coming!'

Then his dad yells, 'Oh Cissie, I'm coming!'

At this the bairn runs in, shouting 'And I'm coming as well, because you're not leaving me with all this debt!'

*

A Vaseline salesman visited Cotemede in Leam

Lane, and went down the entire street giving away tiny wee samples absolutely free. All he asked was that they keep a record of what they used it for, and he'd pop back round with a survey form the following fortnight.

Well, the two weeks passed and he waltzed up to the first front door and said, 'Excuse me, I'm the Vaseline salesman.'

'So you are,' said the housewife.

He asked to what purpose she'd put the Vaseline.

'Medical purposes,' said she. 'My little Jason fell off his mountain bike. His knees were all scraped and I didn't have any Germolene. Then I remembered your free sample, rubbed on some Vaseline and it just did the trick. I'll take three pots please!'

The salesman, well pleased, made the sale and moved next door.

A bloke answered, saying 'You're the Vaseline salesman, aren't you?'

The salesman nodded and enquired, 'And what purpose did you put the tub to?'

'Mechanical purposes,' said the man. 'I've got some machine parts in the garage, and I had nothing to lubricate them with. Then I remembered your free sample, slapped some Vaseline on them, and it worked like a charm. I'll take five tubs.'

Yet another sale was made. The salesman moved on to the next house. As he rang the bell he heard shouting and yelling, children crying, a riotous assembly. A hot sweaty man opened the door, shouting 'Get back' to all the children pushing and shoving inside.

'Excuse me, I gave you a sample pot of Vaseline

a couple of weeks ago. Could you tell me to what purpose it was put?' asked the salesman.

'Sexual purposes,' replied the man.

'What do you mean?' gasped the salesman.

'Well, we've got eleven children, and they run us ragged all day and night. So we've started rubbing Vaseline on the door handle of our bedroom door so the little buggers can't get in!'

*

If you've spent any time in school playgrounds you will know they are synonymous with bad language. One day the teacher asked Terry, 'Who signed the Magna Carta?'

Terry replied 'How the $£&* should I know?'

The teacher was appalled at the boy's gutter language and raced him straight home to his father.

'Mr Jones,' said the teacher, 'I think I must tell you about your son's disgraceful behaviour in school today. I asked him who signed the Magna Carta and he replied "How the $£&* should I know?" '

On hearing this Mr Jones grabbed his son by the arm and said, 'Now come on Terry, did you sign the $£&*ing thing or not?'

*

On arriving in class Miss Tagg discovered a puddle in front of the blackboard with a yellowy colour to it. She was disgusted that any of her class could have done such a thing.

'If the person who is responsible for that doesn't come forward,' she yelled, 'then the whole class will get detention for the rest of the week. I am going to turn my back and I want someone to come forward and write the name of the person responsible on this blackboard.'

This she does and she listens as she hears a chair being pulled away from the desk, the pitter-patter of tiny feet walking to the front of the class, and the subsequent scraping of the chalk. The feet returned to a desk and sat down.

As the teacher turned to look at the blackboard, she spotted a second puddle on the floor, and a message on the blackboard: 'The phantom tiddler strikes again!'

*

Two women in North Shields chatting over the back garden fence. One woman says, 'Last Christmas I had a visit from a strange man with a beard and a sack!'

The neighbour says 'Was it Santa Claus?'

'No,' she replies, 'it was my son coming back from college with his laundry!'

*

The geography teacher, Mr Liddle, asked little Joe what the climate was like in New Zealand.

Joe answered, 'Very, very cold, sir!'

The teacher said, 'Wrong.'

Joe countered: 'What do you mean, wrong? Whenever they send us meat it's always frozen!'

*

Mam and Dad gathered a family conference and declared to their three children that soon they were all going to hear the pitter-patter of tiny feet. The two girls looked at their five-year-old brother and said 'Oh no, William hasn't got dickies again has he?'

*

A primary-school teacher was taking an English

lesson and asked a girl called Carol what 'Can't' stands for.

Carol answered, 'Cannot.'

'Quite right,' said the teacher. 'So what does "Don't" stand for?'

'Doughnut,' came the reply.

*

Sometimes there's an angel on our shoulder. Once I was in an English class, reading a comic, when the teacher picked on me and shouted, 'Robson, name two pronouns!'

Caught off guard, I said, 'Who, me?'

The teacher replied, 'Correct!'

*

If self-abuse stunts your growth, why do they always keep dirty magazines on the top shelf?

*

Is there something malicious in the fact that dyslexia is so hard to spell?

*

My mate Denny was so unlucky as a child that if he fell in a bucket of boobs he'd come out sucking his thumb!

*

Yet another teacher provided me with a lovely remark passed at Hookergate School. The teacher asked a young girl called Karen to name two excuses. Karen replied, 'Me mam and me sister!'

*

The best excuse ever given on a note from parents to cover a young man's absence has to be: 'I'm sorry my son can't come to school today but he has diarrhoea through a hole in his shoe!'

*

I was expelled from school, but it wasn't my fault. I merely needed to go to the toilet, so I put my hand up and asked if I could leave the room.

The teacher said, 'No you can't, just stick it out until break.'

So I did.

*

During the celebrations 50 years on from the D-Day landings, a little lad visited his grandad to ask about the war, as his class was doing a project.

Little Duggie says, 'Granda, have you still got your army helmet?'

The old chap says 'Why aye, it's in the greenhoose full of daffodil bulbs!'

Full of enthusiasm, the little one says, 'Can I take it to school tomorrow to show everybody, please?'

What grandfather could refuse? As he was transplanting the bulbs, the bairn says, 'Have you got some medals, eh?'

Once again the granda nods. 'Aye I do, but you have to look after them, mind!'

So the lad was really getting wound up by now and said, 'Have you got anything else from the war Granda?'

The old fellow thought for a minute and said 'Come to think of it, yes I do. I've still got my old army great coat. It's in the attic over the tank.'

The bairn says, 'Granda, you've got *a tank*?'

*

It was a rush hour and the pacer train travelling from Newcastle to Sunderland was full of commuters. This man took a fancy for a lovely lass standing next to him in the corridor, so he tried to chat her up.

113

'Excuse me,' he said, 'but your perfume is beautiful. What is it?'

'Ysatis,' she replied, 'forty-five pounds a bottle.' She was interested in him and said, 'I noticed you use aftershave too. It wouldn't be Fahrenheit by Christian Dior, would it?'

'Actually it is,' said the man. 'Thirty-eight pounds a bottle.'

At that very moment a horrible smell wafted around the corridor not dissimilar to rotten eggs. Their eyes landed on a little lad who said, 'Heinz beans. Thirty-eight pence a tin!'

HORNIES, BIZZIES, FUZZ, POLISS
AND OTHER CHARACTERS WHAT COME OOT
AFTER YE DIAL 999

Did you hear about the judge who was killed when a boxload of contraceptives fell on him? He was condomed to death!

*

There was a riot at Durham jail and all the prisoners were sitting on the roof, hurling tiles down at the assembly of prison officers and police. They waved banners, tore up wood batons and smashed windows, shouting abuse all the while and complaining about conditions.

Then a man in an anorak squeezed through the fanlight window and started writing things in a tiny notebook.

A prisoner said, 'Hello, are you from the *Daily Mirror*?'

The bloke said, 'No!'

'The *News of the World*?' asks the inmate.

The man shook his head.

'Well, you must be from the *Sunday Sun* then?' continued the old lag.

'No,' replied the man.

115

'OK, I've got it. You're from the *Daily Star*!' said the prisoner.

'I'm not,' said the chap, as he continued writing things down in his notebook.

The prisoner tried the *Daily Mail*, the *Observer*, the *Guardian*, *The Times*, *Cosmopolitan*, the *Sunday Sport*, the *Independent*, the *Evening Chronicle*, the *Evening Gazette*, the *Journal* and even the *Hexham Courant*, and each time the man denied it.

The chap just continued walking around the prison building, which had been totally destroyed, and under his breath he was saying, 'Two hundred Jewson bricks, two hundred Jewson tiles, two hundred Jewson planks of wood . . .'

*

Did you hear about the Teesider who was arrested for carrying out illegal haemorrhoid operations? He got six months and they confiscated his ferret!

*

A lady from Thornaby called the 'Night Owls' phone-in with a story about her dotty mother, whose name is Rose. They were visiting the Kielder Forest when the daughter said, 'Isn't that wood beautiful?'

Rose replied, 'I don't know, I can't see it for trees!'

*

One sunny day in Durham city a student was on the river in one of the rowing boats. Due to his drunken state he completely forgot about the wier, and the boat swept straight over the top, throwing the lad into the river. Fortunately a nearby fisherman spotted him and dragged him to the riverbank, and there he lay, his shoulders on the shore and his legs still in the water. The fisherman knew there was no time to lose, so he began pumping on the student's chest and cranking his arms up and down. The water poured from his mouth, and as the fisherman worked hard to save him a crowd gathered. The more the fisherman pressed his chest the more water gushed from his mouth. A student watching all this yelled, 'Let me through, I think I can save him!'

The fisherman said, 'Why, are you a medical student?'

'No,' answered the man. 'I'm an engineering student, and unless you pull his bum out of the water you'll drain the river!'

*

It was the local North Eastern derby match, and Sunderland had beaten Newcastle in the play-offs. On the way back from the match a Macam (a Wearsider) was so chuffed he was a bit heavy on the accelerator, and as his speedometer hit 95 m.p.h. a blue flashing light appeared in his rear-view mirror. So the Sunderland fan pulled into a lay-by, closely followed by a jam-sandwich traffic car. The Macam beckoned the poliss to his car and held up a card bearing the legend 'DEAF AND DUMB'.

So the policeman wrote a message on his note-pad: 'Please breathe into this bag'.

Then the Macam reached into his glove compartment and after fiddling about pulled out another card that read 'ASTHMATIC'.

The policeman started scribbling on his pad and handed another message to the motorist. 'You'll have to give me a blood sample then!'

Once again the Macam dived into his glove compartment, sending Polo Mints, handkerchiefs, cassettes and sweetie papers flying in all directions. Eventually he surfaced with another sign: 'HAE-MOPHILIAC'.

The poliss was getting well frustrated and scrawled another message: 'I want a urine sample then!'

The Macam was straight into the glove compartment again, to return with another card: 'SUNDERLAND SUPPORTER'.

Think about it!

*

The North East is brimming with history, more Roman ruins, castles, sites of historical interest than any other part of the British Isles. And whenever there is a clamp-down on speeding motorists I wonder if this happened in those days when there were only chariots on the road. Can you imagine a chariot speeding down John Reid Road in South Shields when suddenly a white chariot with an orange stripe across it appears, with a slave waving a blue torch and yelling 'Ne Na Ne Na Ne Na!'

The big poliss Roman pulls the chariot to the side of the road, walks up to the speeding charioteer and says, 'In a bit of a hurry are you? Now let's have your name bonny lad!'

The charioteer says, 'My name is Horatio Xerxes Laetes Idomeus Aentis Asclepius Iphicles Pericles Monoceus Memnon Philoctes Octavius Tndarius Hylas Caesar, Junior!'

The poliss looks at his notebook and replies, 'I'll let you off with a warning this time!'

*

Did you know that chemical weapons were invented

118

in the North East? Every Christmas schoolkids rub snowballs in dog poo before throwing them!

*

Ram-raiders, all wearing stocking masks over their faces, attacked a camera store in the Metrocentre. The police are looking for three men who look like Bob Hoskins.

*

If a girl with briefs is a barrister, what is a girl without briefs?
  A solicitor!

*

She was only a prostitute's daughter but she was streets ahead of her mother.

*

The Northumbria Police tell us that it takes a thief only fifteen seconds to take a radio out of a car. If this is true, why does it take a trained motor mechanic at a garage up to two days to put a new one in?

JOKES I DIV NOT LIKE . . .

What do you call a Geordie in a suit?
  The defendant.

*

What do you call a Geordie in a big posh house?
  A burglar.

*

What do you call a Geordie in a university?
  Lost.

*

There was a little old bloke having a half at his local pub on Shields Road in Byker when a thug walked in. He had a huge beer belly, a yard between the eyebrows, and he dragged his knuckles along the pavement behind him. Without any reason he karate-chopped this old man on the back of the neck, knocking him off his seat. He gave the barman two pounds and told him to buy the old man a drink when he regained consciousness. 'Tell him that was a chop from a 1987 black belt!'

The following night the thug was in the same pub swigging down a bucket of Exhibition, washed down with a bottle of vodka as a chaser, when the puny little old man walked in and hit him across the back of the neck.

The thug fell down like a sack of hammers as the old fellow handed two pounds to the barman and said, 'Buy him a drink when he comes round, and tell him that was a starting handle from a 1954 Morris Minor!'

*

Once upon a time the three bears came home after their walk in Plessey Woods. Baby Bear goes up to the dinner table and says, 'Who's been eating my porridge?'

Then Mammy Bear goes up to her lunch and says, 'And who's been eating my porridge?'

'Stuff the porridge,' says Daddy Bear, 'where the hell's the video?'

*

Big Eck from Kenton had a rottweiler, and was a right so-and-so. He liked nothing better than to find some innocent dog-lover, and set his dog on their pet. He had been responsible for thousands of horrible attacks which some pets had not survived. Big

Eck thought he was such a clever lad, but everyone else saw him for what he was – an utter get!

One day he spotted a man walking his dog on the playing field at Cowgate, so he gets his rottweiler and heads off to confront them. On nearing the owner he looked at this stupid-looking dog. 'Who ye, your dog's ganna fight my dog or I'll chin ye!' barked the yob.

The owner tried to talk his way out of it, but all to no avail. His dog was happily rolling in the grass, and soaking up the sun, when the thug unleashed his rottweiler. The yob laughed, 'My dog will make mincemeat of your dopey-looking mutt!'

Yet as soon as the rottweiler reached the pet, there was a snarling, a snapping and an agonised yelp, and there on the grass lay the rottweiler – dead!

'Bloody hell,' said Big Eck, 'I can't believe that a stupid-looking dog like that could beat a sixteen-stone rottweiler!'

The owner replied, 'If you think he looks stupid now, you should've seen him before I shaved his mane off!'

*

'Can I help you?' said the telephone operator.

'Yes,' said a Geordie voice in panic, 'get me Interpol quickly!'

The operator replied, 'Look, you need to be put through to the International Operator.'

'Oh, very well,' returned the voice. They gave him the number and he dialled again.

When the phone was answered, the caller yelled, 'Is that the International Operator?'

'Yes,' answered the disembodied voice.

'Quickly,' he yelled, 'I must be put through to Interpol. It's very urgent!'

The International Operator enquired, 'Do you have the number?'

'No,' barked the man, 'but hurry! I must speak to Interpol!'

The operator replied, 'You'll have to speak to the Paris Directory Enquiries. Look, I'll put you through.'

'Thank you,' said the man, 'but hurry! I must speak to Interpol!'

There was a longish pause, then a French voice answered, saying "Allo, can I 'elp you, caller?"

The man practically screamed, 'Yes, quickly, I need the number of Interpol. Can you put me through? It's urgent!'

'One moment, *monsieur*, the number is Paris 289777. I shall connect you!'

The caller heard the ringing tone, then a voice replied, "Allo 'allo 'allo!"

'Is that Interpol?' yelled the Northerner.

'*Oui, monsieur!*' came the reply.

'Thank heavens for that,' said the caller. 'Listen, I want to send a bunch of flowers to me mam!'

*

The telephone rang at the fire station. 'Is that the fire brigade?' enquired a rather posh lady's voice.

'It is, hinny,' replied the fireman.

The lady continued, 'You see, I have just planted these flowers . . . '

'I think you must want the flower shop, pet,' interrupted the fireman.

'Some of these flowers are very expensive. My front bed cost almost £800,' she continued.

122

'As I said,' attempted the fire officer, 'you want the flower shop, pet!'

'No, I don't,' barked the woman. 'My neighbour's house is on fire and I don't want you lot trampling over my new flowerbed when you come to put it out!'

*

Singles clubs exist all over the North East. At a famous one on the coast there's a lass who is absolutely desperate for a man. Her name is Gladys and she is becoming increasingly close to her sell-by date, so she tries her arm with every new visitor to the pub.

One day a chap in his forties appeared and ordered a drink, and she was there in a flash. 'I haven't seen you here before,' said Gladys, with as near a pout as her false teeth could muster.

'No,' replied the bloke. 'I've just got out of prison.'

'Really,' said Gladys seductively. 'How fascinating. And what did you do?'

The man looked her full in the face with mad staring eyes and said, 'I killed my wife, I killed my family. I hacked them to pieces with an axe, then I parcelled up the pieces and sent them to convents all over Britain.'

'I see,' said the woman. 'So you're single?'

*

How does an intruder get into your house?

Intruder window!

*

STOP ACCIDENTS – Start doing things on purpose!

*

123

A policeman spots a car rocking down a lovers' lane, so he taps on the window, and a dishevelled bloke winds down the window of his Metro.

'What are you doing in there?' asks the poliss.

'Er, nothing!' says the man.

The policeman says, 'Well get out and let a man in!'

*

Five Tykes from Yorkshire were in a motor accident.

Mr Dear lost an ear.

Mr Clegg lost a leg.

Mr Brand lost a hand.

Mr Singer lost a finger.

Mr Lilley's marriage broke up soon afterwards.

*

There's an infamous lovers' lane near Rowlands Gill and a passing police car noticed there had been a car parked down there since lunchtime. It was now five minutes to midnight, so they drove up to investigate.

As they reached the vehicle they looked inside. The man was behind the steering wheel reading a classic horror book called *Grisly Trails and Ghostly Tales*, and there was a young girl sitting in the back seat knitting.

The policeman said, 'And how old are you, young lady?'

She looks up and says, 'In five minutes I'll be sixteen!'

*

There was an accident – a major pile-up – next to the Granada Services in Washington. A soft-fruit wagon dunched with a lorry transporting sugar, causing a truck full of garden turf to jacknife into both vehicles. A police spokesman said 'Jammy sods!'

*

There were two peanuts walking down the Bigg Market when one was a salted!

*

The North East was the first area to take to unleaded petrol, and in its early days the fuel was said to be prone to burst into flames. This was borne out after a motorist filled up in a garage on the outskirts of Ashington and spilled some petrol on his sleeve.

Well, the driver rubbed as much off as he could, and sped off towards work. Halfway he decided to have a cigarette, and clicked his lighter. The flames caught the petrol on his sleeve. In blind panic the driver wound down his window, put his foot on the accelerator and thrust his hand out the window, hoping that the wind speed would extinguish the flames.

The police just happened to spot him, pulled him over and threw a blanket over his sleeve.

The driver thanked them, and was about to go on his way when the police sergeant said, 'Where do you think you're going. You're under arrest.'

The driver was stunned. 'What for?'

The sergeant grinned, saying, 'Possession of a firearm!'

Star Turn

ALEX ROLAND

One of radio's rising stars, Alex Roland is currently knocking them dead on his hit show 'Hits Not Homework' and is well on the road to becoming a teen idol, having for many years been bone idle. He's a great lad, full of fun, and most people agree he's going all the way.

A man was trapped on Gosforth High Street during the rush hour and there were cars ignoring the speed limit and roaring past him. The man saw a tiny gap and stepped out, only to have to jump back on the path as a motorbike almost mowed him down.

He waited a moment or two and then tried again, and once more had to leap back to the kerb as an Astra skimmed the kerb, doing almost 60 m.p.h. in a 30-m.p.h. zone.

This went on for almost twenty minutes, and he was on and off the road like a jumping jack. A traffic warden spotted him and tapped him on the shoulder, saying, 'I've been watching you trying to cross the road, don't you know there's a zebra crossing down the street?'

The man replied, 'Well I hope he's having better luck than I am!'

A CROSS TO BEAR

When I was little I always thought that God lived in our netty (toilet) because every morning when my sister was in there my dad would hammer on the door and say, 'God, are you still in there?'

*

Three nuns were walking along Jesmond Road in Newcastle. The traffic noise was appalling as rush hour neared. One of the nuns was describing with her hands the tremendously large grapefruit she'd seen while on holiday in Florida.

The second nun proceeded to describe with her hands the gigantic bananas that she'd seen when she was in Jamaica.

The third nun, being a little deaf, said, 'Father who?'

*

Why did God make man first?

Because he didn't want a woman looking over his shoulder!

*

After Lot's wife was turned into a pillar of salt where did he keep her?

In the cellar!

*

Who had the first motorbike in the Bible?

Moses – the roar of his Triumph could be heard throughout Israel.

*

Who was the first tennis player in the Bible?

Joseph – he served at the Pharoah's court.

*

Who drove the first car in the Bible?

God, because he drove Adam and Eve out of the Garden of Eden.

*

Where could you buy the first sweet and sour chicken in the Bible?

From Judas's Carryout.

*

A grasscutter was trying to tidy up the lawns around the cliff face at Tynemouth when he walked just too close to the edge and tumbled over. With a feat of almost superhuman agility he twisted around to grab a damp tree root about a yard from the 200-foot drop.

Despite being an atheist all his life, he cried out to God to help him. There was no reply.

'Help, if you really do exist God, help me now!' he screamed.

Suddenly a voice from above boomed down, 'I am here.'

'Well divvn't just stand there, give 'is a hand then!' yelled the grasscutter.

The voice said, 'All you have to do is have faith!'

The grasscutter's hands were beginning to slip as he said, 'All right I have faith, just help me!'

Once again the voice replied, 'You must have real faith in me, my son!'

'You're on!' he screamed. 'Owt you like, just help me!'

At that God said, 'If you have faith you'll let go of the branch.'

There was a pause, then the grasscutter yelled, 'Is there anybody else up there?'

*

What's black, white, black, white, black, white?

A nun falling down the stairs.

*

A bonny Scot dies and goes to heaven, and he knocks on the Pearly Gates and St Peter is waiting there with his Filofax full of names.

'And what is your name?' asks the saint.

'My name is Angus McIntosh from Duns.'

The saint shakes his head, saying, 'I'm sorry Angus, but you can't come in.'

Angus is clearly shaken; he's lived a good life, helped others, given all his money to the poor, never smoked, never touched alcohol, never ever had sexual contact with anyone. To his knowledge he's never sinned, so he grabs the saint by the shroud and says, 'Just hang on a minute. Why can't I get in here?'

St Peter replies, 'We're not making porridge for one!'

*

A young priest from the Derwent Valley ran off with a seventeen-year-old girl, and after a frisky ravish in a Stanley haystack, the girl looked up and said, 'That would have been our finest hour . . . if it had lasted another 55 minutes!'

130

*

What is black and white and can tell the Pope to get stuffed?

A nun who's just won the pools!

*

With Adam and Eve it wasn't the apple on the tree that ruined them – it was the pair on the ground.

*

Adam and Eve are standing in Paradise when he looks down at his fig leaf rising, turns to Eve and says, 'Get back pet, I divvn't know how big this thing gets!'

*

Who was the first gambler in the Bible?

Adam, because he had a bob or two on Eve!

*

Why did the monk move out of England when Alfred the Great was on the throne?

There was too much Saxon violence!

*

A PRAYER
Dear Lord
In Heaven I have no fear.
I always know that you are near.
I follow your law, your word I teach.
But can I have that blonde on the beach?

*

Why did Adam get thrown out of the Garden of Eden?

For Eve's dropping!

*

Mary and Joseph were riding their donkey to Bethlehem. They couldn't afford a bed and breakfast, so they dossed down in a stable. Mary looked up at her hubby and said, 'Joe, surely there must be some way we can make a little prophet?'

*

A Muslim parachute instructor was putting his pupils through their paces at the airstrip in Brampton. The latest batch had done well, and were just about ready to take their first jump for a vast variety of charities. As the plane revved up they all hopped aboard, and as they climbed to 20,000 feet Frankie from Blaydon shouted, 'What happens if my parachute doesn't open?'

The instructor says, 'All you must say is "Allah help me", and he will protect you!'

So out they leap into the void, and one by one the chutes opened, tugging the jumpers back up into the clouds for their slow descent. All except Frankie! He tugged at his chute but it refused to open, so he remembered his spare and yanked at the ripcord, only for it to come off in his hand!

He looked down as the ground accelerated towards him, and then he remembered what his Muslim friend had recommended. He was travelling at about three hundred miles an hour, but despite the force of the fall he screamed 'Allah help me!'

Within a split second a huge hand appeared out of the clouds, catching the Blaydon skydiver less than ten feet from the ground, and then placed him gently on the ground.

Frankie felt himself, but he was totally unharmed. 'Thank God for that,' he said.

The huge dark hand reappeared and squashed him flat!

*

There's a cocktail on sale along Newcastle's quayside

132

called The Exorcist . . . because it's supposed to bring out the Devil in you!

*

A young lad visited Durham Cathedral and asked the verger about the long lists of names on plaques throughout the building.

'That's a list of the men who have died in the service,' he was told.

The lad tugged his sleeve. 'Was that the eight o'clock or the ten o'clock service?'

*

The North has countless spiritualists, and at one meeting in Houghton-Le-Spring, Ivy was worried about her husband. He'd been dead three months and had always promised that he'd make contact with her after he passed away to let her know he'd made it to heaven.

So the medium began contacting her spirit guides to locate Ivy's husband, Davy. After various grunts, moans and squeaks a voice boomed out, and to Ivy's amazement it was Davy.

'Hello, what's gannin' on?' shouts the late Davy Broon.

'Davy, is that you pet?' shrieks Ivy.

'Hello snugglelumps,' came the reply.

She giggled. 'That's my Davy all right. Are you OK there in the afterlife? What's it all like?'

'Why pet, it's geet canny good as owt!' Davy replied. 'The sky is much bluer, we've got nee pollution, the air is crystal clear. The fields and hillsides are completely green, and covered with trees, the lakes are all a beautiful azure blue, and teaming with fish.'

'Eeh, that sounds lovely pet,' chipped in Ivy.

Davy continued, 'The way of life is so gentle here, all we do all day is eat, make love, sleep, eat, make love, sleep, over and over again!'

His wife was sobbing, saying, 'Thank God you made it to heaven!'

'Heaven?' says Davy. 'I'm not in heaven . . . I'm a rabbit in the Lake District!'

*

A faith healer turned up at Chopwell Community Centre and people from Ebchester, Stanley, High Spen and Rowlands Gill gathered, just in case he could cure them of their wide variety of complaints.

The faith healer walked into the congregation saying, 'What is your name, friend?'

The startled man looked up, saying, 'My name's Frank, and since I broke my legs in a car crash I haven't been able to walk without crutches.'

The faith healer says, 'Rise up, and get on to the stage and go behind the curtain, for using the power that God has given me, you'll be cured this very day!'

So Frank struggled manfully to climb the three steps to get on to the stage, and swung himself around the curtain that stood at the back.

Next the faith healer turned his attention to a sheepish-looking bloke standing near the door. He thrust a finger in his direction shouting, 'I am ordered by God to help you!' The man turned a shade of purple as the healer called to him, 'Come to me young man, and what is your name?'

'Ahm called Pewwy, and a weally want to talk without wolling my words!' said the poor lad.

'Perry, this is the day your sins will be cleansed

134

and your troubles are over!' The faith healer grasped his arm tugging him towards the stage.

The faith healer ordered the congregation to pray hard for the two souls now behind the curtain. He was shouting and yelling, whipping up the crowd into a frenzy of prayer and positive thought. When he stopped shouting you could hear a pin drop; the silence was deafening.

The faith healer said, 'Fred, what I want you to do is feel my power running through your body. Now throw your left crutch over the curtain!'

The crowd gasped as the crutch flew over the top, then burst into spontaneous applause, many yelling out 'Hallelujah!'

The faith healer quietened them, saying, 'Now Fred I want you to feel my power coursing through your veins. Now throw away your other crutch!'

There was a moment's hesitation and then over came the other crutch.

The audience roared their delight. The faith healer silenced them again, and as the hall returned to silence he boomed, 'Now Perry, I want you to feel my power, and speak to me, loud and clear so everyone can hear the miracle that has taken place!'

There was an expectant hush, then Perry said, 'Fwank's fallen off the stage!'

*

A drunk staggered into the confessional at a Catholic church in the Morpeth area. The priest entered his side of the booth, and waited for the man to speak. After five minutes he hadn't said a word, so the priest coughed politely to make the drunk aware of his presence.

Another few minutes passed and still he hadn't

135

spoken, so the priest coughed even louder, still to no avail.

Finally the priest decided to give a firm knock on the partition, at which the drunk shouted, 'Listen, it's a waste of time you knocking, there's no paper in this one either!'

*

A pastor from North Tyneside spent almost forty minutes in the pulpit decrying Sunday opening, then realised that he had run out of wine. He sent a colleague to Sainsbury's to buy some.

*

The vicar of a church in Middlesbrough was giving one of his congregation a firm talking-to, because he was not contributing enough money to the church. 'I'm sorry,' said the gadgy, 'but with the recession I've got so many debts the money just doesn't go around!'

The vicar was not impressed. 'Just remember that you have a debt to God too!'

'I know,' said the man, 'but he's not sending me threatening letters like the others are!'

*

An elderly lady from Pickering had a pet spaniel which was her only companion and one day it died peacefully in its sleep. So she tootled along to a Baptist church to ask if the minister would give a special memorial service and funeral to her spaniel Poppy.

The minister was furious. 'Madam, we do not give services for dogs here in the Baptist church. No, never. I am sorry, but no!'

The lady looked saddened, saying, 'That is a

shame, as I was going to donate £20,000 for the service in the dog's name.'

'Hang on a minute,' says the Minister, 'you didn't tell me the dog was a Baptist!'

*

A priest and a rabbi were sharing a train journey from London to Newcastle. And they were chatting about faith when the rabbi noticed the priest's collar and enquired, 'Why do you wear your collar backwards like that?'

The priest answered, 'That is because I'm a father!'

The rabbi grinned, saying, 'Well, I am the father of two strapping boys, yet I don't wear my collar that way!'

The priest chuckled, adding, 'You don't understand, I am the father of my congregation of two thousand.'

The rabbi gasped. 'It is your trousers you should wear back to front, not your collar!'

*

The same priest and rabbi were chatting as the train roared through Durham. The rabbi could not believe that this handsome priest had remained celibate, and insisted that he must have had sex.

Finally the priest shook his head, saying, 'Yes, I admit it, I have sampled the pleasures of the flesh!'

The rabbi laughed, saying 'It's better than pork, isn't it?'

*

John Lamb came out of Murphy's Bar with two black eyes and a bloody nose. His pal Steve said, 'What happened to you?'

John said, 'I cracked this joke about the Pope to Jimmy McCreery, and he hit me with a chair!'

Steve said, 'You wally, didn't you know that Jimmy is a Catholic?'

'Yes,' replied John, 'but I didn't know the Pope was!'

*

Basil and Bob from Tyneside decided they would hitchhike to the Vatican to see the Pope. By the time they got there they had completely run out of money, and were getting pretty hungry.

They pitched their tent on a lawn near the Pope's residence, and bedded down for the night.

The night was filled with tummy rumblings, and morning arrived with pangs of hunger so severe that something had to be done. They stuck their heads out of the tent just in time to watch an Italian milkman drop off a pint of milk on the Pope's step.

'Basil,' the wide boy said, 'that'll do us,' and off he went running towards the doorstep.

He had just reached the milk bottle and picked it up when the door opened, and there stood the Pope in his white robe and Pirelli slippers. Bob watched in horror, then saw the Pope cross himself. Basil placed the milk back on the step and returned to the tent.

Bob was gobsmacked. 'Basil, that was incredible. The Pope caught you red-handed nicking his milk, and he crosses himself and blessed you. What a really holy bloke!'

Basil said, 'He didn't cross himself and bless me. He said "Oi you, put that milk down and take that tent and bugger off!"'

*

It was Alfie's first day in heaven and he was being given a guided tour by an angel. As they passed all the different places the angel was saying, 'Over there is the area for the Muslims, right next to the Hindus, at the far end of this cloud there's the Catholics, then the Mormons. The Protestants are down there and the Buddhists at the far end.'

At the end of the track Alfie spotted this really high wall, and he pulled at the angel's cassock, saying, 'What's ower there, kidder?'

'Sssssssss,' said the angel. 'That's the Jehovah's Witnesses. They think they're the only ones up here!'

*

Why do Salvationists object to fornication?

They're frightened it will lead to dancing!

*

The local vicar from Sunderland was asked by a women's group if he would give a talk on sex, and he readily agreed. It was then he remembered that his wife was insanely jealous, and decided to tell her the talk was to be on sailing. That night he gave the talk to the ladies and it was a great success.

The following day the vicar's wife was pushing her trolley through Tesco's when the leader of the Women's Institute spotted her and dashed up, gushing over the vicar's interesting talk.

'Thank you for letting your husband give us such a fascinating talk last evening,' said the lady.

The vicar's wife replied, 'I was really surprised that he gave a talk on that subject. I mean he's only done it twice – the first time he was sick and the second time it blew his hat off!'

*

Tommy grabbed hold of his wife's thigh, whispering, 'Howay upstairs and let's make mad passionate love!'

His wife Pat said, 'I'm sorry I can't – it's Lent.'

Tommy replied, 'Who to and for how long?'

*

In America the church welcomes all denominations . . . tens, twenties, fifties.

*

The old fellow was on his last legs, tucked into his bed, and on the verge of crossing the great divide. The vicar stood over him saying, 'Well my son, have you made peace with God?'

The old man's eyes opened and he said, 'Actually we've never fallen out!'

*

The Catholic priest was talking to his friend the rabbi, and they were teasing each other, the priest saying, 'Come on Rabbi, when are you going to have a nice juicy bacon sandwich with me?'

The rabbi said, 'At your wedding!'

*

A Jewish lad once wrote to me at the *Sunday Sun*, complaining that the Christians had stolen the Ten Commandments from his faith. That might be true but he couldn't say that we kept them all!

*

An atheist is someone with no invisible means of support.

*

Once as I hosted a late-night radio phone-in show an evangelist was spouting off about how cunning the Devil was. So I suggested that maybe if the Devil was as cunning as he said, he could be calling himself God. The evangelist was shocked and it led to a juicy night of discussion.

After the show an elderly little old lady rang me and said, 'God will kill you tonight, you'll crash your car on the way home!'

A very Christian attitude, I thought!

*

A young lass from Whickham visited her priest in confession and said, 'Father, forgive me, I've just had sex with a man!'

The priest gasped, saying, 'And was it against your will, child?'

The lass replied, 'No, Father. It was against the wardrobe!'

*

The priest's next 'customer' was a young man who said, 'Father, I'm a milkman and today I made love to Dorothy Thompson, and she was the only woman on my round that I hadn't had.'

'You swine of a man,' barked the priest, 'and what kind of Catholic do you call yourself?'

'Oh I'm not a Catholic,' said the man. 'I just had to tell someone!'

*

Jim Moore from Newcastle was walking along the road when he pulled a hat off an old lady, kicked a dog, swore at a traffic warden, nipped a girl's bum then spat in the gutter.

'Jim,' shouted a neighbour, 'what's wrong with you?'

'Nothing,' came his reply. 'It's just I'm going to confession and I'm short of material!'

*

Rita from South Shields went to confession and

said, 'Father, forgive me. Over the past two days I've had sex with Mark, Steve, Alex, John, Dave, Giles, Maurice, Neil, Mick and Alan.'

The priest said, 'You must take a lemon and suck it for an hour.'

Rita said, 'Will that purge me of my sin?'

'No,' said the priest, 'but at least it will take the smile off your face!'

*

Who was the first trade-union official in the Bible?

Moses – he came back from Mount Sinai and said, 'Lads, I've got some good news and some bad news. I've managed to talk him down to ten commandments, but adultery is still in!'

Star Turn

FRANKIE HOWERD

I have been particularly lucky with some of those famous folk that I've managed to capture over the years. I bumped into Frankie at one of Newcastle's top hotels and he was a fine and courteous gentleman. What you saw on stage is what he was off stage. After a chat and a drink he drifted in and out of a variety of stories and anecdotes. My favourite was this one written as I caught it in Howerd-speak:

Richard decided he was going to become a Trappist monk. The Abbot Francis was in charge . . . yes . . . Francis, you see . . . in charge, yes! 'We are a very strict order,' he said. 'You must live a life of severe discipline! You are allowed only two words every five years!'

So Richard agreed and at the end of the fifth year, he entered the Abbot's office and delivered his two-penneth. 'Bed's hard!'

The Abbot said, 'I know, my son, but that is part of the discipline. Go back and fulfil your duties!'

Five years later the Abbot sees him again and

says, 'Well, my son, what are your two words to me now?'

Richard says, 'Food bad!'

'Yes,' said the Abbot, 'but we are a poor monastery, we must eat what we can afford. So back to work!'

So another long five years went by and once again it was Richard's time to talk. This time his two words were, 'I quit!'

The Abbot says, 'That's fine by me, you've done nothing but complain ever since you got here!'

IT'S FRIDAY NEET,
LET'S GAN TI THE TOON

Brenda from Kingston Park, was fitted with a contraceptive coil before she went out on the town for a razzle . . . Now she's expecting a baby in the spring.

*

A truck driver was looking forward to a night out when his lorry was caught in the usual Gosforth High Street bottleneck. Roadworks and a car crash kept him sitting in his cab for nearly two hours. He was outside the baker's and there in the window was the most beautiful cake he'd ever seen. It was covered with icing, strawberries, and hundreds and thousands. The longer he waited the hungrier he got and finally he decided to hop down from his cab and buy it.

He ran into the bakery and said, 'Excuse me pet, but I fancy that gattux ye've got in your window!'

The snobby manageress said, 'Sir, this is Gosforth, and that is pronounced *gateaux*!'

The bloke says, 'Well, how much is it, like?'

The manageress checked and replied, 'It's twenty pounds a slice!'

The driver said, 'Bolleau to that!'

*

After a few bevvies the lads ended up in a greasy café and the waiter came to take their order, all the while with one hand down the back of his trousers scratching away.

One of the lads shouted, 'Have you got haemorrhoids?'

The waiter replied, 'Sorry, only what's on the menu!'

*

My mate Denny's honeymoon was a total disaster. He discovered she couldn't play darts, pool, poker or billiards.

*

Two punk rockers were walking across old Eldon Square and one said to the other, 'What would you do if a bird plopped on your head?'

His mate replied, 'I'd finish with her!'

*

What does a Bigg Market girl do after sex?

Open the car door.

*

Two Geordies at Dunston Excelsior Club and one says, 'Hey my body is aching all over. It even hurts when I lift up my pint glass!'

His mate says, 'Well, have you tried drinking two halves?'

*

My mate Denny's wife has found an easier way to save money. She spends his!

*

Three pieces of string went into a pub. Two sat

down and one went into the bar and said, 'Three pints of lager and a bag of crisps please.'

The barman said, 'I'm sorry but we don't serve string.'

The piece of string told his pals, and another piece of string got up to give it a try.

'Three pints of lager and a bag of cheese and onion, my host if you please!'

Once again the barman said, 'I've told you lot, I don't serve string!'

At this the third piece of string got up and said, 'Leave this to me lads, I'll sort this prat out!'

So he went into the toilet and tied himself in a neat bow and then ruffles his hair up. Out he stepped straight up to the bar and said, 'Give me three pints of lager and a bag of crisps!'

The barman looked at him suspiciously. 'You're not one of those pieces of string are you?'

The piece of string replied, 'I'm afraid not!'

*

Why do Northerners say 'I'm just popping out for a quick pint', when they really mean a slow couple of gallons?

*

Did you hear about the masochist who liked a cold bath in the morning, so he had a hot one?

*

What do the yuppie Durham Ras (students) chant at football matches?

'Here one goes, Here one goes, Here one goes!'

*

Why do Low Fell girls only have a half-hour for lunch?

If they stayed out longer they'd need retraining.

My mate Denny says that chasing girls isn't one of his failings – in fact he's quite good at it!

*

My mate Denny used to have a girlfriend, but I kept letting the air out of her!

*

Geordie drunks do have a drink problem . . . Two hands and only one mouth!

*

A group of lads were out at a top floating nightclub.
    One said, 'I spent all last night playing cards with my girlfriend.'
    His pal said 'Poker?'
    'No,' came the reply. 'I just groped her a bit!'

*

Two girls were leaning up against the bar at a Quayside pub and one said to her friend, 'I know he's stupid but as long as his wallet stays thicker than him, who cares?'

*

At a Newcastle nightclub a lad walked up to a beautiful blonde getting down to Right Said Fred and said, 'Excuse me pet, but do you want sex?'
    The girl was shocked and said, 'No I do not!'
    So he replied, 'Well, do you mind lying down while I do?'

*

My mate Denny scored with this lass who told him to bring some protection. He came in with two policemen!

*

On the anniversary of his first year of courtship Peter sent his lady a bunch of flowers through the

148

post. She was thrilled and decided to do something special for him when he came home from work.

She moved the bed downstairs, covered it with rose petals and lay there naked in front of a roaring fire.

He opened the door to see his lady in the buff on her flowery bed.

'This is for the flowers,' she said.

'Blimey,' says Peter, 'have you not got a vase?'

*

After picking up a tasty brunette in a Seaburn pub, Les took her for a drive along the seafront. Then the girl coyly said, 'Would you like to see where I was operated on?'

Les gasped, 'I should say so!'

'OK,' said the girl, 'turn left at the traffic lights, the hospital is on the left!'

*

Ritchie from Ryton was out with his brand-new girlfriend when the car ran out of petrol on purpose as he tried to investigate her underwear. 'Out of petrol, eh?' she said. 'What a shame. I was going to invite you back to my place for sex!'

*

The Northern rivers are regular hosts to ships from all over the world, and one weekend a Russian vessel docked on the River Wear.

Two dockers, Bill and Stan, were sitting having a quiet pint of Guinness. As they supped a group of sailors from the ship came in and started downing gallons of bitter. It was Bill's round so he got up and walked up to the busy bar surrounded by all these sailors. He shouted back to his mate ''Arf a

Guinness Stan?' and the Russians kicked his head in!

*

It was late on a Saturday night and there was a huge drunk sitting on a Metro train and he was about eight feet tall and two yards wide. Scrawny Simon sat opposite. He'd had far too much to drink and suddenly he was sick all over this gigantic drunk. He was on the last Metro of the evening and was still miles from home, so he couldn't escape. At that very moment the drunk started waking up, and Simon said to him, 'Do you feel better now?'

*

A girl once told my mate Denny that he reminded her of a junction on a motorway . . . a right turn-off!

*

As Jayne from Burnopfield danced to KLF in Julie's nightclub, a drunken nugget staggered up to her to attempt his latest clever chat-up line.

'Who ye,' he slurred. 'How di ye like ya eggs in the morning?'

Jayne replied 'Unfertilised!'

*

I said to my mate Denny that I tend to put weight on only in certain places. He said, 'You mean restaurants!'

*

An inventor from Murton has created a microwave fireplace. You can spend an entire night relaxing in front of it in just eight minutes!

*

The wild posse from Newbiggin by the Sea loved their Saturday nights, when they all went out for a good drink, then collapsed back to the house to sleep it off. The only problem was 'Big Johnny', who was always sick. He'd been sick on their thick pile carpet, in the jacuzzi, in the toaster and in the fish tank. The lads began to plot how to stop him doing this every ruddy week, and came up with a plan.

They said to him, 'Johnny, one day you'll be so sick your guts will come up, and it'll serve you right, you pig!'

Johnny didn't bat an eyelid, merely belched and swigged down another pint. So later on he staggered home, and crashed into a chair, being sick down the front of his suit as he did so.

At that very moment the lads took out a couple of packets of turkey giblets from the fridge and poured them down his front. Full of beer they all drifted into sleep, and the next morning Big Johnny was cooking some bacon sandwiches and some runny egg on toast.

'Hey fellows,' said Johnny, 'you were right. Last night I did bring my guts up! But thanks to the grace of God and these two fingers I managed to swallow them all down again!'

*

My mate Denny once came home from the club early one night to find his wife kissing the milkman. 'What are you bothering with him for? We owe the coalman £50!'

*

In which month do Northerners drink least?
February.

*

Tom the fiddle player was drinking his fifth glass of

151

whisky in a bar in Consett when the local parish priest says, 'Tom, you shouldn't drink that, it's the Devil's brew. Let me show you something!'

So he popped out into the pub car park, ferreted between the hedgerows and returned with a worm. 'Watch this,' said the priest as he dropped the worm in Tom's whisky.

Slowly the worm contorted and died. 'See,' says the priest, 'does that not tell you something?'

Tom said, 'Yes, it tells me as long as I drink whisky I'll never suffer from worms!'

*

My mate Denny told me that I should never, ever visit a strip show, because if I ever did I would see something that I shouldn't. So one day I did visit one, and saw something I shouldn't – him!

*

Joe and Jimmy popped into a restaurant close to Newcastle Playhouse. When the waiter delivered the soup his thumb was deeply dipped in it.

Then he brought the main course, curried chicken, and once again the waiter had his thumb in it. The sweet course followed, custard and apple pie, and as ever the waiter's thumb was buried in the custard.

Jimmy was well angry, saying, 'Why don't you learn to keep your thumb out of people's food? It isn't hygienic!'

The waiter replied, 'I have arthritis in my thumb, and the doctor says I have to keep it warm.'

Jimmy was appalled that he'd done this on purpose, and says, 'Well, why don't you stick it up your bum then?'

The waiter walked away, saying, 'I do when I'm in the kitchen!'

*

At a restaurant in Seahouses, Michael and Jayne went for a meal to sample the fabulous seafood, particularly the restaurant's speciality – lobster. It was duly delivered on a bed of rice, but Michael noticed it only had one claw.

'Excuse me,' said Michael, 'what happened to this lobster's claw?'

The manager replied, 'Well, the lobster had obviously been in a fight and lost the claw, sir.'

Michael said, 'Well take it back and bring me the winner or I'll dab you!'

*

I visited a restaurant in Newcastle's China Town and ordered a special chicken dish. Well, I got a mouthful and it was so badly undercooked you couldn't eat it. I just chewed and chewed and chewed but couldn't get it down.

I called the waiter and said, 'This is rubbery!'

The waiter said, 'Thank you very much!'

*

Rory from Rothbury walked into a posh restaurant in Northumberland and said, 'Excuse me but does your cook have turkey breasts?'

The waiter said, 'Yes he does, but don't worry – he has a T-shirt on!'

*

At a big show at the Sunderland Empire my mate Denny had the beautiful girl dancers hammering on his door . . . he wouldn't let them out!

*

Colin from Leeds took his girlfriend down a

renowned lovers' lane. She wound the windows down and said, 'Isn't that beautiful? Listen to those crickets chirping!'

They were actually zips but he didn't have the heart to tell her!

*

My mate Denny was making passionate love to a midget from the Hoppings, the biggest travelling fair in Europe, when his wife walked in on them. 'Denny you swine,' she yelled, 'you promised me you wouldn't be unfaithful to me!'

Denny said, 'Howay, can't you see I'm tapering off?'

*

Rob came home early from work to find his best friend's BMW parked outside his house, so he crept in and heard the telltale noises of passion from the upstairs bedroom. He sneaked into the garage, got his shotgun from his locked cabinet and stealthily headed upstairs.

He dragged the bedclothes off them as his best mate leapt out of bed stark naked. Rob put the barrel of the shotgun towards his mate's groin, saying, 'You turncoat, now I'm going to blow your private parts off!'

'Please, Rob,' pleaded his pal, 'we've been mates for years, give me a chance!'

Rob says, 'OK, swing them!'

*

Alex went out on his stag night and one of his friend's pranks went badly wrong, trapping his cheeky bits in a mousetrap. He was rushed to a doctor who bandaged it up and put four splints on it. Rather than worry his bride-to-be, he chose to keep the mishap quiet and merely wore baggier trousers for the wedding.

After the reception he found himself alone with his fine blonde beauty of a wife. She was wearing her most seductive Damart underwear and slingback wellies – how could any man resist? He was getting undressed when she said, 'Alex darling, do you know that you are the very first man to make love to me? My body has not been touched by anyone else!'

At that moment Alex dropped his pants and said, 'You can talk. Look at this, it's so brand new that it's not even out of its box yet!'

*

Paul was the boss, and his wife had been nagging him for months and he was using this as an excuse to work an extra hour each night. Well, it was a Friday and his secretary had agreed to work late too. He buzzed her, saying, 'Andrea, do you have any paracetamol? I've got a splitting headache.'

Andrea checked her bag then replied, 'I'm sorry Paul, I haven't, but I just live two minutes away. Why don't you pop around before you go home? I'm sure I've got some there.'

So Paul popped to her flat, and after some aspirin and a few drinks, he was well relaxed, and one thing led to another. Following an afterglow nap, Paul woke up in Andrea's bed with a start, looked at his watch and saw it was 1.20 a.m. His wife had expected him six hours earlier.

He explained how he really had to rush home and asked, 'Andrea, have you any talcum powder?' She nodded and brought him a container of Boots' best. He spread it all over the arms of his suit then headed home.

As soon as he got through the door he saw his wife standing there, her teeth out and her curlers in.

Women look awful with a mouthful of curlers.

Paul then told her how he'd gone back to his beautiful secretary's flat and made crazy wild love to her several times before falling asleep in her arms.

She eyed him up and down and said, 'Don't you lie to me. Look at that chalk on your jacket, you've been up that ruddy snooker club again haven't you?'

*

A Geordie called Malla came home early to find a man in bed with his wife. 'What do you think you're doing?' he shouted.

His wife said, 'Don't worry Malcolm, he's a doctor and he says he's just taking my temperature!'

Malla picks up the breadknife and says, 'Well, all I can say is that thing better have numbers on it when you pull it out!'

*

My mate Denny has had twelve wives . . . mind, only one of them was his own!

*

Young Jack from Ashington spent six months in Switzerland, where the locals called him the 'Geordie Gigolo' because of his reputation with the ladies. Photographs of his waxed moustache and eyebrows were avidly collected by women across Europe.

A Swiss woodcutter was terrified that young Jack would visit his home and ravish his four beautiful

156

daughters, so he decided to vary the times that he would return home from work.

On Monday he came back at four o'clock, only to see a blurred shape skiing away from his mountain chalet. He raced to the house and burst inside to see his eldest daughter's bedroom door kicked down, and she sitting there cuddling a red rose and a photograph left by the Ashington Romeo.

'My first daughter has been taken advantage of! I will kill that swine of an Englishman!' he snarled.

The following day he returned an hour earlier. He was a hundred yards from his door when it burst open and Young Jack skied straight past him, knocking him into the snow. On getting to his feet he rushed inside to find two doors kicked in and his two eldest daughters sighing heavily, cuddling Jack's photograph and looking longingly at the single-stemmed red rose he had given each of them.

'Damn him,' screamed the woodcutter, 'he's ravished my two eldest daughters. I'll kill him!' And he took his shotgun to work with him the very next morning.

He finished at two o'clock, and was at his front door kicking the snow off his snow shoes when he heard moaning noises from inside. On opening the door he saw Jack on skis leaping out of a bedroom window. He fired a shot, missing Jack as he zoomed into the snow.

The woodcutter saw all four of his daughters' rooms had been visited. He yells at Jack, 'You have just ravished all four of my daughters!'

Jack yodels back, 'And your-little-old-lady-too!'

*

Two Benwell lads meet up in heaven and they're

talking about how they got there. Alan explained that he had frozen to death. Billy said that 'I had been suspicious that my wife was having an affair, and I cut short a business trip so I could catch her in the act. I was too late, he had just left, but I found his black jeans and polo neck shirt and his bright red jacket. So I decided to leave my wife, but she would get nothing of mine. So I started throwing all of the appliances out of the window. I chucked the stereo, the video, the TV and the compact-disc player down to the street. Then I lifted up the fridge and it was so heavy that I slipped and it pulled me out of the window and I fell a hundred feet to my death.'

Alan said, 'It's a shame you didn't look in that fridge, because if you did we'd both be alive today!'

*

A brain goes into a pub and the barman says, 'I'm not serving you, you're out of your head already!'

*

Why is going to see strippers just like looking in your rear-view mirror?

You're bound to see someone's behind!

*

During a pub quiz the questionmaster asked Ingrid to name the three most important parts of a man's body. She says, 'The first is the brain, the second will be the heart . . . and the third must be . . . the third thing must be . . . Eeh! I've had it just at my fingertips . . . it's been on the tip of my tongue. Honestly, I've had it drilled into me a thousand times. No, I can't remember!'

*

Why do Northern yuppies drive BMWs?

Because they can't spell Mercedes.

*

What's the definition of a yuppie with a social conscience?

He buys a holiday cottage in Scotswood!

*

What do you call a happy yuppie?

Yippee.

*

My mate Denny sold his house last week. When the council find out they'll go mad!

*

Duggie, a farmer from Felton, married another farmer's gorgeous daughter. On their wedding night he said to his new bride, 'Come on Sally, get your clothes off and get into bed with me right now!'

Sally says, 'I'd love to, Duggie, but I'm afraid I've got the woman's monthly.'

Duggie wrinkled his brow, saying, 'So what? I've got the *Farmers' Weekly* but I'm not going to read it now!'

*

Charlie was bragging that his wife could still get into her wedding dress 25 years after they were married. He forgot she was eight months pregnant on their wedding day!

*

Women are like the continents.

Between 14 and 18 they are like Africa, mostly virgin and partly explored.

Between 18 and 24 they are like Australia, highly developed and well built up in all the important places.

159

Between 24 and 30 they are like America, with great technique and always seeking new methods.

Between 30 and 35 they are like Asia, hot, sultry and mysterious.

Between 35 and 55 they are like Europe, devastated but still interesting in places.

Between 55 and 120 they are like Antarctica – everybody knows where it is, but nobody wants to go there!

MIKE NEVILLE, MBE

When Mike won his MBE I was thrilled to bits and whistled down in the car to give him a bottle of champagne, as he really is a great performer. His lady wife once helped out in a charity bash I was involved with for 'War on Want' and I've always had time for them.

Once during another charity do, recording a song called 'Try Giving Everything', Mike and I teamed up to sing all the flat notes. It was filmed on video at Newcastle City Hall and to keep us cool they passed around a huge glass wellie filled with beer. It stopped at Mike, and it took a great deal of persuasion to get it back.

We had worked together before with his old pal George House on a comedy album called *Radio Jarra Slax*.

This white horse goes into a bar and says, 'Giz a bottle of broon, Jack!'

'Hey,' says the barman, 'd'you know there's a whisky named after you?'

'What,' says the white horse, 'Eric?'

*

'Now come on Alan,' says Mike, 'you didn't say it had to be funny!'

QUESTIONS
YOU'VE NEVER BEEN ASKED
AT A PUB QUIZ

Is a *pas de deux* the father of twins?

*

If a plug doesn't fit do you socket?

*

Does fishing result in net profits?

*

Is a budget a baby budgerigar?

*

Are Japanese babies called nipples?

*

Is it true that when the nugget put his condom on backwards he went?

*

What do you give a cannibal who's late for dinner?
  The cold shoulder!

*

Why is it a waste of time to write to Washington?
  Because he's dead!

*

What did the VD bacteria say as it fell off the cliff?
  I'm a goner'ere!

*

What's the definition of macho?
Jogging home from your vasectomy!

*

What's big and black and sails the seven seas?
Bin Bag the Sailor.

*

What happened when Moses went to Mount Olive?
Popeye nearly killed him!

*

What do you call ghosts who go to raves and take Ecstasy?
High spirits!

*

Why don't nuggets have ice cubes?
They've forgotten the recipe!

*

What do you do when you see a drunk with the shakes in the bath?
Throw your washing in!

*

How have the Smurfs survived the recession?
They sell their excrement as Blu-tack.

*

How do dinosaurs pass exams?
With extinctions!

*

What's white, furry and smells of mint?
A polo bear!

*

What's green, round, smells of vinegar and pecks trees?
Woody Woodpickle.

*

How do you make a potato puff?

Chase it round the garden!

*

Why did J. R. Ewing go to court?
  To Sue Ellen.

*

What's green and sits in the corner?
  A frog in a huff!

*

Why was 6 scared?
  Because 7, 8, 9.

*

Why did the girl have her hair in a bun?
  Because she had her nose in a cheeseburger!

*

If a little lad can play piano by ear, can older boys
fiddle with their privates?

*

Where do ships go when they're not very well?
  To the docks!

*

What happens to cabbage white butterflies when
they fly in the rain?
  They get wet!

*

Which King of England was a milkman?
  Alfred the Crate.

*

What do you call a rich teddy bear?
  Winnie the Pools.

*

Two teddy bears in the airing cupboard – which one
is the Scotsman?
  The one on the pipes!

*

165

Two teddy bears in the airing cupboard – which one is in the army?

The one on the tank.

*

Two flies on your wallpaper – which one is the bandit?

The one heading for the border!

*

Two fleas on a bum – one flea says to the other, 'I haven't seen you for ages, where have you been?' His mate says, 'I've been in the nick!'

*

Two flies sitting on a dog turd – one fly says, 'You're not looking too well, what's the matter?' 'Nothing,' says the other fly. 'I've just come off the sick!'

*

Two puddles of sick were walking down the street when one puddle says to his pal, 'I was brought up around here!'

*

What did the nugget say when he saw a hundred elephants walking over the hill?

'Look, there's a hundred elephants coming over the hill!'

*

What did the nugget say when he saw a hundred elephants walking over the hill wearing sunglasses?

Nothing, he didn't recognise them!

*

What do you call a man with no hands who can play the piano?

A right clever dick!

*

What do you call Postman Pat when he gets the sack?

Pat.

*

There were two pencils who liked to chase women. Which one didn't catch any social diseases?

The one with the rubber on!

*

Why did the man put a packet of Daz on his TV set?

Because he had no Ariel!

*

Why are football pitches always damp?

Because people keep dribbling on them!

*

What is deadly, very dangerous but incredibly slow?

Caustic Skoda.

*

Who was the poorest cowboy in the West?

Skint Eastwood.

*

How do you make a coat last?

You make the trousers first!

*

What do you get if you cross a motorway with a shopping trolley?

Knocked over!

*

What's pink and hard first thing in the morning?

The *Financial Times* crossword!

*

What instrument did ancient Britons play?

Anglo-Saxophones.

*

How do you spot a feminist?
  Flick bits of paint all over her!

*

What's the difference between a sewing machine
and a female jogger?
  A sewing machine only has one bobbin'.

*

What's a vampire's favourite song?
  'Living in a Box'.

*

What do you get if you cross a girl from the *Sunday
Sport* with a packet of Bisto?
  Gravy with very big lumps!

*

What clothes do musicians prefer?
  Chords!

*

What's yellow and goes 'SLAM, SLAM, SLAM,
SLAM!'?
  A four-door banana!

*

What's green and gets you drunk?
  A giro!

*

How do you get rid of moles on your legs?
  Hit them with a rolled-up newspaper!

*

How do you make a cigarette lighter?
  Take the tobacco out.

LINDISFARNE

The most famous of all of the Northern super-groups, and a great bunch of lads. I started singing in pubs and clubs using their tunes, but fortunately they survived. We worked together on a charity record called Geordie Aid, and they were with me for the grand switching on of the Christmas lights in Newcastle Upon Tyne.

Alan Hull was raised in Suttons Dwellings in Benwell, the next street along from me, and once he fell down the stairs with an entire crate of brown ale and didn't spill a drop. He kept his mouth closed.

On asking for their favourite story Ray Laidlaw came up with this corker:

'There are hundreds of tales relating to life on the road,' he says, 'mostly of the "sex and drugs and rock'n'roll" variety, but I think this tale gives an insight into the wit and wisdom of the travelling musician, regardless of the type of music played.'

Jimmy Shand and his Scottish Country Dance Band

were performing for a week at a large, swish country hotel in the Highlands of Scotland. The discounted rate the hotel was prepared to offer Jimmy for accommodation for the band was a lot more than Jimmy was prepared to pay. After much fruitless negotiation he booked his rather miffed band into a cheaper local bed-and-breakfast establishment. The digs were particularly spartan and the breakfast served to them on their first morning caused another outbreak of grumbling in the ranks. It was the custom of the good lady of the house, Mrs McTavish, to provide a couple of slices of dry toast and boiled eggs that were so small they couldn't have been provided by anything larger than a sparrow. This type of 'jockey's rations' did not go down at all well with a potentially mutinous band who had been looking forward to living it up in the posh hotel for a week. The band persuaded Jimmy to have a word with the landlady to tell her to provide something more substantial for their breakfast and at least to have something to spread on their toast!

Mrs McTavish wasn't too pleased about this request as she felt she was feeding the band adequately, bearing in mind the small amount that Jimmy was prepared to pay. Reluctantly she agreed to see what she could do about the situation.

The band came down to breakfast the next morning with high hopes. Their optimism soon evaporated when they observed that the table was set with the usual minuscule eggs and dry toast. There was one addition, however: on a silver platter in the centre of the table was a tiny pot of honey, the one-portion size that is usually provided on planes or in cafés.

The band looked at each other with a mixture of amazement and hilarity when they realised that this tiny pot of honey was the only tangible result of Jimmy's negotiations with the landlady.

At this point Mrs McTavish came into the room with a smug smile on her face, obviously thinking that she had got the measure of these impudent musicians. The band all turned to Jimmy, waiting for him to respond to the pathetic improvement in their diet. Jimmy then delivered the *coup de grâce*. He picked up the tiny jar of honey, turned to the landlady and said, 'Good morning Mrs McTavish, I see your husband keeps a bee!'

GILES SQUIRE

Giles started his career as a DJ on small-scale shows and has worked his way up to senior presenter, and onwards to become programme controller of Metro FM. Not only that, but his skill and expertise has given the radio station an audience of 52 per cent of the population of the North East; and he created the hit show 'The Europarade' that discovered thousands of hits long before the rest of the country. Giles has given us a tale from the Scottish Borders.

It was a misty night at Glencoe, where the eerie-shaped mountains stand like a fortress to hold back those that would dare trespass upon Scottish territory.

The English army was on the march to stem the Scottish rebellion, their red coats stretching for miles as their commander Sir Roger Rushton sat astride his horse in front.

171

Just as the soldiers were about to enter the valley a strange voice echoed down to them. 'Stop there ye Sassenach scum. 'Tis I, Angus McFee of the Clan McFee. I think ye's are a cowardly lot. I say that I, wild Angus of the Glen, will be able to defeat any two of your men!'

Sir Roger laughed and sent off two of his most burly and vicious troops to sort out this upstart of a Scot.

They never returned!

Ten minutes later the voice boomed out again. ''Tis I, Angus McFee from the Clan McFee, and those Sassenachs were nee match for a Highlander. I could beat any dozen!'

So at once Sir Roger ushered his men into the valley with their sabres drawn.

They never returned!

''Tis I, Wild Angus McFee of the Clan McFee. You don't think these useless excuses for men would stop me? They're cowardly curs, ignorant swine and no match for me! Your fancy soldiers can't defeat one single Scot!'

At this Sir Roger, rapidly losing his patience and losing his men, sent in a hundred of his crack troops to flush out the rebel and kill him.

They never returned!

This went on, and each time Sir Roger doubled the number of men until he had sent 800 soldiers.

Each time they never came back.

All that were left was Sir Roger's elite private guard, 1,000 troops, so he decided to march into the mists of Glencoe and deal with this boastful Scot himself.

He was almost a hundred yards into the valley

when there, staggering towards him, came one of his men. He was bleeding from the head, bleeding from the arms, bleeding from the chest, bleeding from the legs and he was convinced his haemorrhoids had started up as well. He slumped at the feet of Sir Roger's horse.

Dismounting to be at the man's side, Sir Roger opened his hip flask, and let the wounded man sip at his brandy.

He coughed and spluttered, and tightly grasped the commander's lapel.

'Don't go in there, sir,' said the man. 'It's a trap!'

'What do you mean?' said Sir Roger. 'A trap?'

'There's two of them!' replied the soldier!

GET YOUR RODS OOT FOR THE LADS

To me fishing is a sport with a worm at one end and a dummy at the other, but we have some of the finest fishing in Britain in the North. Some of our lakes are so full of fish they have to swim standing up. My dad used to take me fishing, where I'd sit with a line in the river for twelve hours without ever catching anything. Still, I suppose it's better than just sitting around doing nothing. Whether this is a jerk at one end of the rod waiting for a jerk at the other end, it matters not. One of the biggest, if not *the* biggest, hobby sport in the world deserves some room, so let's go down by the riverside.

An American was boasting about a fish that he'd caught in one of the rivers that feed the Lake District. 'It took me close on three hours to land the fish. Once we'd got it out of the water I realised it was too small, so me and four of the other guys threw it back!'

*

Why did the sand cry?
Because the sea weed.

How can you make a turtle fast?

Don't feed him.

*

John and Jack were sitting on the banks of Kielder
Reservoir and fishing to their hearts' content when
a hearse and funeral cars drove along the nearby
road. John stood up and took off his fishing hat,
holding it over his heart. Jack says, 'That's really
canny of you John, showing such respect for the
deceased!'

John replied, 'Why, you know it's the least I
could've done. We were married for over thirty
years!'

*

Why are sardines stupid?

Because they lock themselves in tins and leave
the key outside.

*

Two fishermen are in a leaky rowing boat in the
middle of the River Coquet, it's bucketing down
with rain, they are covered in thousands of midgie
bites, their food is ruined due to the leak, and they
are soaked to the skin, coughing and spluttering.
One lad says to his mate, 'Keep reminding me how
much fun I'm having, will you!'

*

A fishing rod is a long stick with a hook on one
end and a liar on the other!

*

Maurice was fishing off the end of Seahouses pier
when he overbalanced and fell in. Half a dozen
fishermen ran to his aid, lobbed him a rope and

pulled him around to the dock where he climbed up the ladder.

'How did you come to fall in?' asked a bloke.

The fisherman said, 'I didn't come to fall in, I came to fish!'

*

Two lads were in the Bacchus in Newcastle, planning a fishing trip. Peter said, 'I'll bring the boat and motor, and I'll fill her up with petrol!'

'Champion,' said Davey. 'I'll bring the lunch then!'

So the next day Peter pulled up outside Davey's house in his Ford Granada, tugging a trailer with the motorboat. He opened his boot so that Davey could put his stuff in the back. First he chucked his rod and bait in, then started humping a crate of brown ale, two twelve-packs of lager, a bottle of sherry, half a bottle of whisky and six cheese sandwiches.

Peter said, 'Hey come on, we'll never eat all them sandwiches!'

*

What robs all the fish in the pond?

Dick Terrapin.

*

What do you call a lobster who won't share his dinner?

Shellfish.

*

What do you get if you cross Charles Bronson and a haddock?

Death Fish.

*

In the pub Jimmy was bragging that he had never

caught a small fish. Everyone was sick to death of him going on and on about how good a fisherman he was. Finally his pal says, 'So you've caught some big fish have you? Well I've caught a much bigger fish than you! In fact, the photograph of it weighed twelve pounds!'

*

Many Southerners don't believe that the fishing is so good up North, but one day on the River Aln a Londoner walked up behind a fisherman to see his keep net bulging with trout, bass, roach and salmon.

'Do they bite?' asked the Cockney.

'Do they bite?' said the fisherman. 'When I bait the hook I've got to hide behind the car!'

*

Hexham riverside is beautiful on a hot summer's day and my mate Denny was there fly-fishing. The fish were really teasing him, nibbling the bait then swimming off, and Denny was getting more and more frustrated as he kept trying to hook them.

'Bugger, I've missed!' he shouted after yet another fish escaped.

A local priest overheard him and said, 'Listen, young man, you must not blaspheme like that. If you continue surely God will strike you down with a bolt of lightning!'

Despite his newly found Catholicism Denny kept on fishing, and once again a sizeable fish managed to avoid his hook, but took his bait.

'Bugger, I've missed,' cursed Denny.

The priest was getting angrier. 'Look I've warned you, if you swear one more time, God will strike you down!'

Denny paid the priest lip service but was far too

involved with his fishing to stop. Then a fish at least two foot long took his bait and missed the hook, as Denny tumbled backwards into the water. He stood up, his waders full of water, and shouted, 'Bugger, missed again!'

The blue sky clouded over and rumbled ominously. There was a crack of thunder and a flash of lightning fired down and completely incinerated the priest.

God stuck his head through the clouds and said, 'Bugger, I've missed!'

*

It was the big fishing tournament near Corbridge and all the lads were taking their catches up to be weighed. Terry was there with a string of fourteen minnows. He looked at the bloke in front who had a salmon over his shoulder almost four feet long. The bloke looked around at his string of minnows and grinned, so Terry said, 'Only caught the one then?'

*

Barry and Alan were out fishing and Barry was catching a fish every single time he cast into Bolam Lake. Alan was more than just exasperated and said, 'How do you know exactly how to cast to catch a fish every single time?'

Barry explained, 'It's simple. When I get up in the morning, if my girlfriend is lying on her right side, I fish from the right side of the boat. If she's lying on her left side then I fish from the left side of the boat!'

Alan asked, 'And what if she's lying on her back?'

Barry grinned. 'Who the hell's going to go fishing?'

*

Why are men better swimmers than women?
They've got rudders!

*

X-CERTIFICATE

The following jokes are rude, bawdy and entirely in keeping with the sense of humour that abounds in the North East. I implore you not to read on unless you have a mind so open that the wind whistles through it. I don't want to use swear words, but the jokes are fairly explicit. So div not say you was not warned! They might be naughty but they are funny!

*

When Sunderland FC won their way to the FA Cup Final against Liverpool in 1992 there was an awful lot of hassle getting hold of tickets, thus a lot of Macams from Wearside fell into the hands of the touts. One lad from Pallion was outside Wembley, trying to find himself anyone with a ticket to sell, when he spotted a tout.

'You're wasting your time, son,' said the tout. 'I've sold all my tickets, but I've still got mine. I tell you what. If you give me £100 I'll let you have it!'

'A hundred pounds,' said the Macam. 'I could buy a woman for that!'

The tout says, 'Yes you could, but would you get

45 minutes at each end and a brass band in the interval?'

*

A little old lady walked into a record store in New-castle and asked the assistant, 'Have you got "Jingle Bells" on a seven-inch?'

The assistant had gone a bit overboard at the Christmas party and replied, 'No, but I've got jangly balls on a twelve-inch.'

The little lady asked, 'Is this a record?'

The assistant replied, 'No, but it's not bad for a sixteen-year-old!'

*

It was breakfast time at the convent, and the Mother Superior was giving instructions to her novices as to their duties for the week.

'Sister Rose,' said the Mother Superior, 'you will do the cooking for the week.'

Sister Rose nodded and set about her tasks.

'Sister Brenda,' continued the old nun, 'you will sweep all the rooms, and make the beds.'

The sister picked up her dust pan and brush and off she went.

'Sister Jayne, you will sweep all of the leaves away from the front of the convent and do the gardening,' ordered the Mother Superior.

Then the Mother Superior turned to Sister Andrea and said, 'And you will get into the convent's Mini Metro and go along to Presto's to collect the shopping.'

'Ah, howay Mother Superior,' implored Sister Andrea, 'don't make me do that, I did that a fortnight ago, and it was terrible!'

The Mother Superior was disgusted at this breach

of discipline and said, 'You will do as you're told, Sister Andrea. Here are the car keys, off you go!'

Sister Andrea was well against it, saying, 'But it's that policeman from the village, he's got it in for me, he persecutes me. Every time I go along the road he flags me down and gives me a hard time! Please send someone else!'

The Mother Superior was having none of it, and grabbing Sister Andrea by her surplice, put her out next to the old battered Metro. 'Turn the other cheek, my child,' was her only advice. So off went Sister Andrea towards the supermarket. She was very nearly there and there was no sign of the policeman, so she began to unwind. As soon as she relaxed, there he was, standing beside the bushes, and he ordered her to pull across to the side of the road.

He walked around to the driver's side and said, 'Is this your car, Madam?'

Sister Andrea was already riled. 'Look you know this is not my car, it belongs to the convent, but you know I am allowed to drive it!'

The policeman continued, 'Can I see your driving licence then?'

The young nun replied, 'Look, you saw my driving licence a fortnight ago, and a fortnight before that, and a fortnight before that. Why do you want to see it again?'

'Look,' said the policeman, 'if you just show me your licence you'll be on your way all the quicker!'

So she fumbled around in her bag and finally unearths the licence.

'Can I see your logbook now?' asks the policeman, handing back her licence.

'You saw the logbook last time, and the time before. Why do you have to see it again?' asked the seriously irked woman.

'As I've told you,' said the poliss, 'just let me see the logbook. You're only delaying things!'

So the logbook was found in the glove compartment.

The policeman examined it, then asked to see her insurance.

'This is ridiculous,' screamed the nun. 'I'm just going to the supermarket, why are you harassing me?'

'Just doing my job,' said the policeman. After checking the insurance he added, 'Will you get out of the car please?'

'Look,' says Sister Andrea, 'I got out of the car the last time, and the time before, and the time before that!'

The policeman insisted and she walked around into the bushes where the policeman stood. As she stood there he started unzipping his fly.

The nun screamed, 'Oh no, not the breathalyser again!'

*

Did you hear about the sex-mad pizza salesgirl who forced my mate Denny into making love to her for seven days and nights non-stop? Now he's going to cool it for a while.

*

A young lass called Eve from Northallerton got married but didn't have much dosh, so agreed to 'live in' with her mam. Her new husband was very grateful, and the wedding was a great success. They returned to the mother's house and he turned to his new bride, yawned and said, 'I'm tired. Shall we go to bed, or stay up late and watch *Neighbours*?' Eve blushed, and sent him upstairs, saying that she'd join him presently.

She was really scared, never ever having been with a man, but her mam reassured her, and sent her after him. She was shaking as he got ready for bed. Then she turned and ran back downstairs and grabbed her mam's arm. 'Mother, he's just taken his teeth out, they're false!'

Her mother said, 'A lot of people have false teeth. Don't worry about it, it just means he won't bite you! Go back up to your new husband.'

So off she went again, and within five minutes she was back down. 'Mother, he's just taken one of his eyes out, it's made of glass!'

'Don't worry,' said her mam, 'a lot of people have glass eyes. It means he'll get his glasses half price. So get back up there!'

So Eve went back to the bedroom as he was taking his shoes and socks off. She saw that all the toes on his right foot had been amputated.

She races back downstairs shouting, 'Mother, you don't understand! He's got a foot and a half!'

The mother says, 'Look, you stay down here and I'll spend the night with him!'

*

My dad was reading a Northern sex book called *The Perfumed Allotment* when he spied this phrase: 'Sex is greatly improved for the man if his partner utters low sexy moans during the climax of the carnality'. So my dad decided to ask my mam to do that for him. 'Listen, Audrey pet, next time we make love I want you to moan, but don't you moan until I tell you!'

So my mam agreed to give it a go – it didn't seem tricky, just moaning when he wanted her to. So she put her best flannelette nightie on, and he was already in bed waiting. They began kissing and canoodling and my mam said, 'Shall I moan now?'

'No,' gasped my dad, 'not yet. I'll tell you when!'

So five minutes later, while my dad was in full flow, my mam said, 'Now, hinny?'

'No,' panted my dad. 'I'll tell you when to moan!'

So the moment was fast arriving and my dad shouted, 'Now Audrey, moan pet, moan!'

And my mam says, 'What a day I've had, the sink overflowed, then next door's cat had widdled on our doorstep again, and you don't give me enough housekeeping, and that milkman has been standing on my azaleas and . . . '

*

What do you call a woman who can suck an orange through a hosepipe?

Darling.

*

A little lad was standing in the corner of the plush carpeted office of his headmaster, and while he waited for his turn to see him, he nibbled away at a packet of salted peanuts. He dropped a handful, bent down to pick them up and the headmaster spotted him, saying, 'Jamie, you've got some hairs on your nuts!'

The bairn replied, 'I know and I'm only twelve!'

*

Why do women tend to get piles?

Because God made man a perfect asshole!

185

*

A vicar from a church in the Cheviots was giving his sermon. 'Now, it's funny, this thing we call belief. How many of you believe in ghosts?'

Most of the congregation put their hands up. The vicar continued, 'And how many of you have seen a ghost?'

Nobody raised their hands, so the vicar continued, 'How many of you have ever made love to a ghost?'

To the vicar's surprise, one man stood up at the back of the church and said, 'Me!'

'Good heavens,' said the vicar. 'You have actually made love to a ghost?'

'Oh, a ghost,' said the man. 'I thought you said goat!'

*

What's the difference between an egg, a carpet and a bit of the other?

You can beat an egg, you can beat a carpet but you can't beat a bit of the other!

*

I was giving a talk to a group of biology students at Lancaster University. They had just completed a course on 'Sexuality Around the Globe', so I asked this gorgeous brunette called Karen what she had learned.

'All kinds,' said this dream on legs. 'I learned that Scotsmen are the most well endowed!'

I was surprised and she continued, 'And did you know that Red Indians are better lovers and have greater stamina?'

'I didn't know that,' said I, and then she asked what my name was.

'Tonto McEwan,' I replied.

*

A manipulating bloke from Shiney Row put his wife on the game, and as she was stunningly attractive, business was brisk. So one teatime he returns from the pub and asks his wife to pop upstairs and get his slippers.

'Give me a break,' says the wife. 'I have been up those stairs with 72 different men today!'

The husband says, 'Your poor feet!'

*

Nobby walks into Bensham Library and sees this lady having some trouble reaching a book on the top shelf. 'May I be of assistance, Madam?' he enquired.

'Thank you,' said the woman. 'I was looking for a thriller!'

Nobby looked along the top shelf and asked, 'Do you like Dick Francis?'

'Yes,' she replied, 'but how did you know my name was Frances?'

*

Many, many years ago when I was treading the boards as a singer/comedian I saw David Essex make a guest appearance. He was wearing a white suit, black shirt and had a red rose in his button-hole, and he looked like the star that he was. So when my very first guest appearance as a 'celebrity' came around I had no option than to follow the example he had set. I had been invited to do the gig no one else would accept, the opening of a new sports hall at a private health club in Northumberland. The owners were George and Elizabeth Todd, who were particular fans of my radio show. So having accepted, I tried to get that David Essex look, by asking my mother to make me a white suit, as I couldn't afford to buy one.

On the day, I set off in my mam-made suit and black shirt, a red rose in my lapel, really feeling I looked the part. I took a friend called Neil who carried a portable Uher tape recorder so that he could capture my first 'official opening' to broadcast that evening.

On arriving at the gates I discovered it was a naturist club, and we were very amused, and intrigued. Having red blood in our veins we instantly thought of being surrounded by hordes of beautiful naked women. And me in a new suit! How could I fail?

On getting to the gatehouse, I stepped out of the car to book in and find out where to park. There I met a man in a white terry-towelling dressing gown, who handed me a rack similar to those used in swimming pools and said, 'Just put all your clothes on that, I'll lock it away and you can follow me.'

I explained that I was not a nudist, so therefore I wouldn't be stripping. Neil had decided to wait outside in the car. I told him I had the suit made special, but this was rather like trying to wear a baseball cap at a Ku Klux Klan gathering. It was their way or nothing.

The man pointed at the poster that read 'Metro Radio's Brave and Fearless Flashing Blade opens the new Sports Hall this Saturday'. The sound of my old nickname gave me no option than to remove my clothes. I was wishing I had brought a speech to cover my vitals, but none was to hand, so my vitals tried as best they could to shrink and hide themselves. It was a chilly October day and on stepping from the gatehouse to the inner courtyard, as soon as the wind hit me I shivered involuntarily. My male portion had lost its sausage-like appearance and was now doing the impression of a mushroom in a cornfield. I thought I was changing sex, so I tried to brush it and get a bit of life in the ruddy thing.

This man had a pair of sandals on as he crunched across the gravel pathway, but as for me, in bare feet, trying to walk and look macho, I ended up mincing like a duck tap-dancing on broken glass.

We went in through the rear of the sports hall and stepped out on the small stage.

I had worked thousands of pubs, clubs and ballrooms so had no fear of an audience, but being naked makes you feel totally vulnerable. Still, I thought to myself, how many people in Northumberland would be nudists? Surely no more than a few dozen. A little damage-limitation exercise would do no harm, I thought.

I had learned a comedy routine, and now I went over the running order in my mind until I was as ready as I could be.

Anyone who has worked live a lot can tell roughly how many people there are in an audience just by hearing them. There were far more than a few dozen here. My throat was drying, and it was then that I realised my plight may have been serious but my private parts wasn't being serious at all. To avoid total embarrassment I actually slapped him twice, to restore some degree of normality.

The man removed his dressing gown and walked on to the stage, his fat belly hanging over his naughties. My mam was right – I should've eaten my crusts. He didn't have to slap his best friend, now mine had completely disowned me!

I heard his announcement: 'Here is your very own Flashing Blade, Alan Robson!' It crossed my mind for a split second that maybe it was a set-up; perhaps I was on *Candid Camera*.

Force of habit told my legs to walk on and accept applause from what was a rapturous crowd. My ears strained to hear some of the small children say, 'Mam where's his willy?' Fortunately, if it was asked, I never heard it.

I was about to launch into the jokes and the stand-up routine when my brain finally took in what pictures my eyes were sending. There in front of me were around eight hundred naked people. Every age of man and woman was in attendance, the well-hung and those deserving of a rebate. One universal thing struck me. The older you get the more everything seems to head south. This was 'natural', we were all born in this state, yet nothing felt as un-natural. I had played loads of sport and showered with the lads, but when I see this much flesh, it is totally off-putting. My jokes were merging into one. I realised that the biggest joke there was me!

I started talking, and tried to make eye contact with the audience, yet it became apparent that none of their eyes were focusing on my face. I glanced down; my portion had become interested in what was there and was coming out for a look. This may have made me more respectable, but then I started to panic, thinking he was going to stand up and make an exhibition of himself. Fortunately in my panic he decided to take things easy.

I was about to declare the hall open when the first flash went off. Cameras! I hadn't even considered cameras, yet after the first one it was almost like a strobe. I opened the hall then ran off to the wings to tremendous applause. My act had been very basic – no jokes, just straight business – but I was through with it. After shaking some hands – and it is amazing how everything else shakes when you shake hands in a nudist camp – I got dressed and hurried to the car to speed away.

I kept this gig under wraps, merely mentioning I had opened a 'specialist club', and the story remained buried.

What I didn't expect is that the people who had taken photographs would send them to a 'naturist' magazine. The editor had put a photo about two inches square in a feature about the month's highlights, and some thoughtless so-and-so passed it on to a fellow radio presenter. Well, that weekend I arrived to do the 'Saturday Show' and there, blown up about eight feet square, was a naked Robson. The canteen, the corridor notice boards and the office all had a poster. All over them guests and staff alike had scrawled various jokes. The worst and most humiliating was the canteen poster covered in crosses, and carrying the legend 'Spot the Ball'. No one had crossed anywhere near the right place.

I have since that day always considered this to be the 'David Essex' curse.

The humiliation fermented and bubbled inside me for many years until one evening David agreed to appear live on the show by telephone. He'd always been a tremendous performer, with his hits 'Rock

On' and 'Gonna Make You a Star!', his TV series and his amazing stage shows. I would have fun chatting to him, yet deep down I wanted to pay him back for the way he had 'unknowingly' contributed to my misery.

Fate stepped in during our chat live to over a million people. Whilst he used his car phone David said, 'Hang on Alan, I'm being trailed by a police car, I better not use this . . . Oh hang on, I think he's going to pull me over . . . '

The devil on my shoulder cheered, and I started roaring laughing. David said, 'I don't think that's very nice of you . . . '

Little did he know!

He wasn't booked and the curse was exorcised.

*

My mate Denny ran into his doctor's and shouted, 'You must help me, Doctor. Every time I ravish my wife her toes curl up. What should I do?'

The doctor replied 'Try taking her tights off first!'

*

A fisherman was fishing near Holy Island when he spotted a beautiful mermaid sitting in a rock pool combing her hair with a bright red coral comb. He walked over to this gorgeous creature, whose measurements were 36, 24 and £1.35 a pound.

'Excuse me,' he said. 'Are you real?'

The mermaid nodded.

'Have you ever been kissed by a human?' said the man.

The mermaid shook her head, and the fisherman stepped up and kissed her passionately.

The fisherman then enquired, 'Have you ever had your breasts stroked by a human?'

Once again the mermaid said, 'No I haven't.'

So gladly the man duly obliged, and then he said, 'Have you ever had a man nuzzle and kiss your breasts?'

'No, never,' replied the mermaid, and the fisherman dived to her chest and caressed them. Then he stood up and said, 'Have you ever been had by a human?'

'No,' said the mermaid, her voice all a-tremble.

'Well you have now,' said the fisherman, 'the tide's gone out!'

*

Jackie from Heaton weighed 44 stone and he preferred women bigger than him. At last he found the woman of his dreams and she weighed 56 stone. They were married within the month and soon found themselves at a honeymoon hotel in Ullswater.

He carried her over the threshold – it took four trips – and she lay on the bed and he climbed on top and began kissing her while they ripped each other's clothes off.

'Darling,' said Jackie, 'can I switch the light off?'

His bride looked sad, saying, 'But sweetie pie, if you really love me, you shouldn't want to hide your body.'

'I don't,' said Jackie. 'It's the lightbulb, it's burning me bum!'

*

A rich landowner in Alnwick was looking at his son's expenses. They read:

JULIE – £45

ELSIE – £60

IRIS – £52

DOREEN – £62.

The landowner sent for his son and told him, 'Listen, if your mother was to read this, she'd be really disappointed in you, frittering away the family fortune on women of ill repute!'

'But Dad,' said the son, 'I love having sex with these girls, they really know what to do to give a man a good time!'

'I know,' said his dad. 'Just do as I do. After you've been out with one of them, put the expense down to shooting. Then your mother won't suspect!'

So the following month his father picked up the young lad's expenses again and they read:

SHOOTING – £45
SHOOTING – £60
SHOOTING – £52
SHOOTING – £62
REPAIRS TO GUN – £225

*

I visited Jordan recently on a business trip and stayed at a very posh tourist hotel. I was in a bit of a hurry, and on swinging around I bumped into an American woman, catching her in her chest with my elbow. 'I am most dreadfully sorry,' said I, 'but if your heart is as soft as your breast, then I'm sure you will forgive me!'

The American woman replied, 'And if the rest of you is as hard as your elbow I'm in Room 46!'

*

Explaining to little children about matters of the flesh can prove hazardous. Such was the case when a little six-year-old walked in while his mother and father were making love.

'What are you two doing?' asked the tot.

'Oh,' said the startled father, 'I'm just filling your mother up with petrol.'

'Blimey,' said the child, 'she mustn't do many miles to the gallon. The milkman filled her up this morning!'

*

All of the 'My Mate Denny' jokes in this volume are based on Dennis Ferguson, quite simply the funniest man in the North. He's a great comedy actor but he is his own worst enemy. He is a bagful of emotion: when he's enjoying life he's a joy, but when he's down he's a disaster of religious proportions. He's appeared with Melanie Griffiths and Sting in the movie *Stormy Monday*, he's appeared in countless television plays, and was voted the hit of Gateshead's National Garden Festival. He's appeared as Dr Watson to my Sherlock in *Sherlock Holmes and the Case of the Christmas Curse*, voted by *The Stage* as the North's best panto of 1991/92.

Yet I'm going back to this man's manic past where he had been known to borrow crutches and then tumble down stairs into a pond full of Koi carp in a Chinese restaurant, thus winning a free meal. I go back to when he was the star of a local panto called *The Lambton Worm*. During the interval Denny removed all his clothes and walked along the corridor into the dancing girl's dressing room. There were about thirty shrieks and screams until the company's seamstress said, 'Denny, where are your clothes?'

At this Denny looked down and said, 'I've been robbed!'

Keeping his clothes on is difficult. We worked at Newcastle Playhouse performing a series of sketches loosely based on TV commercials, me playing his straight man, and trying to get rid of him once the impact of each gag had been realised to its full potential. Yet the blood went to his head again. He had brilliantly recreated about a dozen classic ads when Marvin Gaye's 'I Heard It through the Grapevine' began to play, and much as Nick Kamen had done on screen, Denny began removing his clothes and putting them in a spin dryer. The audience howled with laughter. When he reached his underwear that was my cue – I was to stop him, and push him behind a table, where his undies would be covered.

Then we played the 'Hamlet' music and a few puffs of smoke appeared, and the audience cheered and applauded.

It is at this time when Denny is at his most dangerous. The audience were in his pocket, and with a rush of blood to his head he tore off his underpants, hurled them at me and shouted, 'Now how are you going to get me off?'

I hope you have as much fun sharing the great Northern humour in this book as I had collecting it. Enjoy it!

I wish you well

Alan Robson